everyday
legends

'the ordinary people changing our world'

D1393459

the stories of 20 great UK social entrepreneurs

James Baderman
Justine Law

Published in 2006 by WW Publishing
Innovation Centre, Heslington, York YO10 5DG

Designed and printed by the very artistic and patient
Simon Smith and Blush Creative (www.blushcreative.co.uk)

ISBN 0-9550132-1-6

Printed on 100% recycled paper

This is a non-profit-making project between ?What If! and UnLtd.
Any profits made after costs have been accounted for, will
be used to fund more great social entrepreneurs.

Contents

What makes a social entrepreneur?

Put simply, social entrepreneurs are people who want to change the world. That doesn't mean they necessarily develop complex, global solutions to large-scale issues; often, social entrepreneurs simply take a problem in their own community and make a commitment to tackle it. This may lead to something bigger, or it may not; what makes a true social entrepreneur is that they have the will to make a difference, the vision to know how to go about it and the determination to make that vision happen.

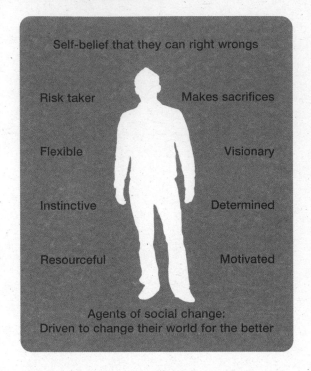

Self-belief that they can right wrongs

Risk taker   Makes sacrifices

Flexible   Visionary

Instinctive   Determined

Resourceful   Motivated

Agents of social change:
Driven to change their world for the better

And what is social entrepreneurship?

Traditionally, 'doing good' has been very much the role of government or the voluntary sector; fully committed people but often bound by rigid and bureaucratic structures. Then you have the business world, for whom doing good tends be limited to 'doing less bad', or writing cheques to charities. We find social entrepreneurship really exciting because it represents those traditionally exclusive sectors beginning to overlap, and the best of all three sides meeting in the middle to approach social issues in new ways.

In that middle space you find social entrepreneurs who can combine the heart and commitment of the voluntary world, the scale and remit of government, and the discipline and dynamic nature of the business sector. We'd go so far as to say this is where the 'nirvana' of social change is at.

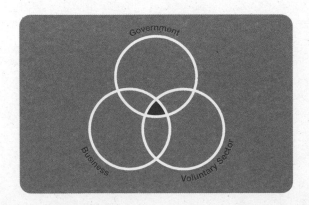

Government

Business

Voluntary Sector

Who we are and why we've written this book

?What If! and UnLtd work closely together on a number of projects, both to support individual social entrepreneurs and to make the world more receptive to social entrepreneurship. We wrote this book because we wanted to inspire people to be as passionate as we are about social entrepreneurship. There are some very impressive organisations funding and promoting the sector, but a lot of what is written we have found to be quite theoretical or academic. We think that to really engage a wide range of people we need to tell real stories and we need to tell those stories in a way that is accessible, human, and not too heavy. So, you won't find any business plans or organisational charts or clever theories on growth, but you will get a feel for the reality of launching a national childcare scheme from your kitchen table, or selling fruit and veg out of a disused council flat.

?What If! is the world's largest independent innovation company, we work with clients who genuinely want to innovate and grow. We work on innovation projects to help clients release the creative potential of their people, products and brands, and we work with clients to increase their innovation capability – this means developing their skills, organisational structures and leadership for successful innovation. We work in over 40 countries worldwide with a wide range of clients and across several market sectors.

?What If! has a team called Footprint which is dedicated to using core ?What If! skills to support social entrepreneurs. Since 2003 we have been helping to step-change the progress of many people and projects like those featured in this book. Footprint is a key part of the company and the culture at ?What If! and we're very proud to be able to have an impact in this way.

www.whatifinnovation.com

UnLtd - the Foundation for Social Entrepreneurs, supports social entrepreneurs throughout the UK. We do this by giving awards which comprise a complete package of funding and practical support; the aim being to give social entrepreneurs the best possible chance of success for their projects. We are unique in that we only fund individuals not organisations; this is because we believe that it is people who have the potential to change society for the better. Our Award Winners are driven by passion; it is our role to help their passion flourish so that they can create tangible projects which can potentially transform communities. In the two years that we have been running we have funded thousands of individuals who have demonstrated incredible vision and determination. UnLtd has around 50 staff in six offices in England, Wales, Northern Ireland and Scotland. We are funded by a £100 million endowment from the Millennium Commission. This legacy is carefully invested so that it generates enough income to fund our awards in perpetuity.

www.unltd.org.uk

We've found 20 great stories from the UK (and a special extra one from the USA), but this is by no means an exhaustive list. We know there are loads more social entrepreneurs out there doing inspiring work, and we hope to have the privilege of helping them tell their stories too one day.

This is a non-profit-making venture; any money we make after meeting our costs will go into a pot and be awarded to the most promising young social entrepreneur we come across in the next year. Of course if lots of people buy the book we can make more than one award!

John Bird

The Big Issue: a magazine sold by homeless people to provide them with employment and a legal income. Profits from the magazine are invested in schemes to help prevent homelessness.

Why he's here...

John has fundamentally changed the way society deals with homelessness. The 'hand up not a handout' principle helps vendors break the cycle of homelessness (unemployment, poverty, lack of structure, low self-esteem, etc.) which many charity-based responses don't afford. The strength of the idea has made The Big Issue an iconic brand, and a way of addressing homelessness across the globe.

?WHAT*IF!* UnLtd*

THE BIG ISSUE

Who is John Bird?

John was born in West London in 1946 to a working class Irish family. He spent much of his childhood living with relatives and in care, and he was held for three years in a juvenile detention centre.

After being expelled from a degree course at Chelsea School of Arts John drifted for a decade until in 1974 he started his own business as a printer and publisher.

In 1991 he launched The Big Issue with Gordon Roddick and has since received numerous awards including an MBE and a doctorate. He has spoken at the UN, 10 Downing Street, Buckingham Palace and Westminster, and advises the government on social exclusion.

The issue he confronted

At the end of 1991 almost 40,000 households in England were 'accepted as homeless and in priority need'.

The solution he's created

14 years after its launch there are now five UK editions of The Big Issue (London, the North, Wales, the South West and Scotland) being sold by around 4,000 individuals. There is a national circulation of 155,575.

Big Issue titles are also published in South Africa, Japan, Australia and Namibia.

The Big Issue leads the International Network of Street Papers which unites street papers around the world.

The Big Issue Foundation uses the profits from magazine sales to fund services for homeless people, including education, training and finance programmes.

In 2003 The Big Issue Foundation worked with over 1,000 homeless or vulnerably housed people many of whom were re-housed, given training and counselling, as well as housing and career advice.

John's story

Being qualified for the job

I'm not much of a businessman, most of my ideas are crap, but I do have a certain staying power. I started life in a London Irish slummy ghetto which was full of poverty, aggression, violence, bad manners, bad parenting, bad culture, bad people. All that stuff that makes you a bit mad. I've spent most of my life trying to get over that poverty and that abject situation, and I've got some scars on my face to show for it.

My family were made homeless when I was five and at seven I was taken in by the Sisters of Charity and put into an orphanage. Between then and starting The Big Issue I spent most of my life being dishonest. I came out of care aged 10 and went shoplifting, housebreaking and nicking cars when I couldn't even reach the pedals. I got sent to a reform retrieve for three years, came out at 18 and went to Chelsea Art College but got expelled. Then I fucked about, got married, made someone pregnant and spent some time on the run from the police and the social security. I went to Paris, became a revolutionary and tried to destroy capitalism (didn't do a very good job). I came back to the UK, got married again, had two kids and became a small businessman in the world of publishing and printing. Although I was an excellent printer I was terrible at the pretty important stuff like invoicing and pricing. 17 years later I started The Big Issue.

Our first move was to present the idea to the establishment homeless charities. Their reaction was: 'What do you know about homeless people? Who are you? Have you got a degree in it? You haven't worked at a shelter through the night, been on a helpline, been on a sleep out, rattled cans in the street, or wiped a homeless person's arse.' I replied: 'I've been homeless, I've been a rough sleeper, and I've had drink, drug and violence problems. Maybe it's time that someone who's had the problem of homelessness was able to get involved in making the decisions'. They were completely bollocksed by that and suddenly started telling me things like their grandfather was a train driver and they always drink India Pale Ale out of a can.

With a little help from my friends

The Big Issue came about when I bumped into an old mate. We'd first met years ago when I was sleeping rough in Edinburgh and I'd started an argument about who had the biggest nose. When we met again in 1987 I discovered that this friend was Gordon Roddick, husband of Anita Roddick. He had started the Body Shop and was now a multi millionaire; I always say never ever let up on a friend who has loads of money.

The Big Issue was Gordon's idea. He'd seen a paper in New York being sold on the streets by homeless people, but it was a very poorly put together paper, a pity paper; people bought it because they felt sorry for the person selling it. He came back to the UK and put the idea to the 'homeless industry' and they all said it wouldn't work; it couldn't work because you couldn't trust homeless people. He got the Body Shop Foundation to fund it and asked me to run it. Because I hated charities and I hated do-gooders, I only agreed on the basis of it being a business, and it would be my business. He gave me the money to start The Big Issue and we launched in September 1991, now it's all over the world.

Not another charity

When we started out there were literally hundreds of charities just in London alone for the benefit of the homeless. I didn't want to do a charity because charities piss me off. The ones I met were full of 'nice' people who were totally sentimental about homelessness and I wasn't interested in sentimentalism because I thought the world was a shit hole. I thought homeless people were treated abysmally, especially by themselves, and that charities were not tough enough to say to homeless people 'Look you're causing these problems yourself. The world screws you over, but you've got to sort yourself out.'

The charities we met were all about giving homeless people another handout rather than giving them the one thing that they needed: opportunity. Opportunity to a homeless person is a job; in fact what keeps most of us from falling to pieces. Work gives you social association, friendships, a sense of responsibility, and the chance of making your own money so that you don't have to ponce off the state and ponce off your parents.

As a charity you can't give work to the dispossessed; you can only be nice to them, and give them some soup and a roll as they sit in their doorway. This isn't opportunity, it isn't even respect: it's a kind of unconditional love normally reserved for little children. It seemed utterly logical to me to give people that have fallen to pieces the thing that keeps you and I sane, and that is work.

Education, education, education...

...the homeless

The first thing we had to learn was how to handle homeless people because they were very violent, aggressive and used to getting away with things. We also had to educate them that we weren't an extension of the handout culture, and we weren't the middle class liberal do-gooders that they had become so expert in guilt-tripping.

So we established a few fundamentals: they had to buy the papers up front otherwise they would have stolen them from us; they had to agree to sell the paper from a particular pitch in a particular way and not be pissed out of their minds or out of it on gear. Equally, if they attacked us then we attacked them, if they spat in our faces we spat in their faces. We had near riots on occasion, but we recognised the one thing that they respected and that was people standing up to them.

Alongside this hard line was also some basic common sense stuff. After the first year we had about £12,000 stolen from us. The money was being kept in the safe by our distribution manager who was an ex-homeless person and he was pissing it up the wall. In the chaos of the early days there was a lot of trust expended in the organisation and we learnt that we had to install some controls; if we had too many loop holes somebody would find a way to rob us. So we didn't set people up to fail, we didn't put temptation in their way.

...the public

Far harder than retraining the homeless was, and still is, persuading the public not to throw cash at homeless people: nothing has done more to create a dependency culture amongst the dispossessed than the indulgent attitude people have to giving. It's almost as if they're walking around with cash in their pockets saying: 'I'm really upset with this pound. But hang on, look there's someone over there who looks sad, and they've got dirt on their face. Here you go…' And even now, with the paper out there making sure homeless people are selling rather that begging, we haven't managed to control that impulse; people want to pay £5 for a magazine that costs £1.40. No homeless person is going to say 'hang on I don't need your money', it's going to make them think that being dirty and living on the street is a sustainable way to make money.

This attitude exists throughout society, even amongst some of the most hard-nosed businessmen. Once a year these guys, the same guys who normally track every penny spent and invested by their organisation, will put on a red nose or a silly hat and prance around like Dopey. They'll then donate cash to a charity which they haven't really investigated. That's schizophrenic. The UK is sick with this desire to give money away and what people don't realise is that if you give something away for nothing you enslave the recipient because you give them a reason to come back again and again.

...The Big Issue staff

If I was doing The Big Issue again I would have never employed any of those people who are in love with the dispossessed. I'd have bought in tougher staff and had them operating a more structured environment for homeless people to come into. I'd almost go so far as to organise philosophy lessons for those

staff around how you intervene and bring about change, and how you can't do it with idealism.

I think this because when we've had people working at The Big Issue who really 'love' and identify with homeless people, the homeless have played around. If you indulge homeless people and give them no barriers or limitations they demand more and more attention like a high maintenance lover.

Being shoddy, but liking it

When you put it all together it's pretty amazing that The Big Issue has survived: it was founded by a 45 year old who had never managed anyone; its sales team is made up of the homeless, who are the most unreliable workforce on God's earth; and unlike a charity we've always been in the market place and therefore have been buffeted up and down by that market. Sometimes we resemble the chaos of a casualty department without enough dressings, but we continually survive and I often think that it's precisely the constant challenges that keep us going.

Over the years there have been countless cock-ups and I would celebrate that. When you've got a mistake you've got something to build on. We've made money and wasted it, tried to do big things that fucked up, invested money in America, bought buildings, sold buildings… If you get it right first time you will never know how you got it right: success with no cock-ups is an innate thing.

I actually think that The Big Issue has always been a bit of a shoddy organisation, and again I would celebrate that. The offices have always been scruffy and rough looking and people have wanted to tart them up, but I've always liked them that way. We're always a bit non-deferential to each other, and I like that too. We've always been just hanging on in there, so there's this sense of fighting the world, and I've always liked that too.

Put all this together and you can get a sense of our particular style of existence. As a result we've exhausted quite a few people who've worked here, but we've also primed several people to go on and do

9

great stuff. We're probably the most well known social business there is, and it's great that lots of people have used The Big Issue as a stepping stone to other charities and social businesses.

Spreading the word

I look upon myself as starting new businesses; I opened a kind of social McDonald's and we've been opening new branches ever since. This is how we've expanded following our success: the latest branch is in Brazil, before that Tokyo and Osaka, before that Namibia and South Africa, before that Gambia, Russia, Germany, Italy, France... Some of these papers have launched under The Big Issue name and some through the International Network of Street Papers which we started in 1994.

More recently we've stretched ourselves a little further with a series of new ventures created to direct people to what we call 'cross road businesses'. We launched Social Brokers which is about finding fundraising for people starting social enterprises, and we've actually raised our own fund called the Big Invest with the Royal Bank of Scotland (and others) to provide funding for social businesses. Rather than just getting The Big Issue all over the place, these businesses get the social business ethic of The Big Issue out there into lots of different sectors and addressing lots of different needs, and so far these new ventures have been a success.

There is also a much wider sense of expansion which really centres around myself. When people think of The Big Issue they think of me, and therefore I'm asked to support and lend my name to a whole range of new ventures. What this does is help the public to make sense of this social business ethic; 'oh, it's like The Big Issue. I get it now'. So in a way this 'sponsoring' of other ventures is a further expansion of The Big Issue brand.

The rewards of being a successful social entrepreneur

If you get together a number of social entrepreneurs they will all be incredibly competitive. There is a big ego element, with people saying: 'I'm going to crack it', and: 'I'm here with a purpose'. What is lacking is the honesty you get in commercial business where people admit that they do it for the money. Alan Sugar does it for the money; if there was no money in it he wouldn't do it.

Social entrepreneurs are caught in a tricky situation: in a sense they're just financial entrepreneurs displaced by the fact that it's no longer right or sexy to be a greedy bastard. So, instead they're evangelical and they've got to make their mark. They dress it up as 'I want to be nice to the world', but in fact their success is down to the fact that they are very competitive and to some extent very greedy people.

I include myself in that; we're greedy for success. We want to be in every newspaper, we want to be the one who 'did it'. The pay back isn't the big houses and the yacht (my missus and I have just got our first mortgage and I don't own anything beyond that), the payback is the kudos. Social entrepreneurs want to be important, they want to be seen, and they want to celebrated. I think it's bad news that we can't be honest about that, that we have this need to dress up that ambition. I think people should say 'Firstly I'm doing this for myself, and great that it might help other people as well'. So, when someone asks me why I started The Big Issue I say 'to help me pay my mortgage'.

So far so good, but still a long way to go...

I was getting in a car one day and this big Scottish homeless guy jumps in the back with me and I think 'oh god, he's going to have a go at me'. His name is Dougie and he says: 'Since I left the army I've been in and out of prison. I used to rush into building societies poor and come out rich. I've always been in trouble and always been violent. Then four years ago I met The Big Issue and since then I've been straight as a die'. This story is fantastic not because of Dougie, but because of the impact beyond him. I did a few rough calculations: it costs about £35K to keep someone in prison for a year, so over four years, by removing one arsehole from circulation, we saved the government £140K which could be spent on something more productive than locking people up. We sent an invoice to the Home Office but unfortunately we didn't get any response.

We've got countless stories like Dougie's, but I still think we haven't come within a mile of our potential and that's my biggest concern. The very idea that you take people who are in crisis and instead of saying 'this is what we're going to do for you' you say 'what are you going to do for yourself?' is really revolutionary and of course could go way beyond homeless people. If you took The Big Issue concept and used it in a doctor's surgery, a school, in nutrition... actually getting people to take responsibility for their issue, that's the potential of The Big Issue, and it's huge.

But we also need to be a bit honest; our intervention into the lives of homeless people is not without its issues. A third of the people we help will use the money they earn to stick stuff down their throats and into their arms. This is life, let's not kid ourselves that we can achieve 100%. Another third of our vendors will say: 'ah, I've got a job for life. I can sell 200 papers a week, and I can live off that'. Like all interventions our solution has created a new dependency, and yes it's better than begging, but it's still dependency. We have to find new methods of moving people on.

...and for me

Most of the people at the top of the social business network are idealists and I'm not an idealist. I've had my idealism well and truly beaten out of me. I tried Jesus, I tried Marxism, I tried being a small businessman, and then I tried social business, and now perhaps I've almost got out of that too. What I've become is a kind of political figure spending most of my time trying to reinterpret the over-arching structure of society rather than trying to find another cure.

We do need people rushing around like blue arsed flies finding social cures, but we also need the people who've done that for a few years to take on leadership and to fight the big issues. Why is it we spend so much money on cure and not on prevention? Why do we get so excited about Jamie Oliver, but we don't get excited about the people who prevent him having to go and sort people's food out? Why do we love seeing Jamie in socially deprived areas? If we dismantled social deprivation Jamie Oliver wouldn't have to spend his time sorting out dinner ladies. Virtually all the energy we spend on social justice is spent finding cures and emergency responses, it's never, ever around prevention.

So, we have to make prevention sexy. We have to dismantle the causes of poverty, rather than pick kids up when they're 10 because they've got lice in their hair, when they're 12 because they're committing crime, when they're 15 because they're malnourished, when they're 18 because they're dealing drugs, and when they're 20 because they're in Feltham (Young Offenders Institution). It's unsustainable.

My top tips

"Stop waiting around for the right opportunity to intervene. People ask me 'what can we do?'. Go down to the nearest old people's home and do someone's shopping, clean someone's windows; stop postponing the day when you start changing things."

My call to arms

"Buy The Big Issue, read it and tell us what you think so that we can make sure you buy it every week."

"The Big Issue costs £1.40, so only pay £1.40 for it."

Ideas you can steal

'A hand up not a handout'

Although there are certainly situations where aid or crisis relief are the only way to intervene, society should look wherever possible for long-term, sustainable solutions that give responsibility to people to improve their own lives. The Big Issue really delivered this ideal to the world.

Don't get too comfy

John has intentionally maintained the prevailing stress and tension within The Big Issue. Although this makes the organisation a tough environment, it also means that there is a rich energy and sense of momentum which drives the organisation to make things happen.

Embrace mistakes

The Big Issue has never been ashamed of the mistakes it's made, and this gives staff the permission to take risks and therefore to deliver both an impact and innovation. There are even some companies who have a mistakes fund and demand that it be spent each year!

Be brave

Throughout John's story are accounts of jumping in, having a go, and sometimes plain and simple blagging when the shit hits the fan. Being comfortable taking risks, both as an individual and as an organisation is what separates real innovators from the rest.

Reed Paget & Marilyn Smith

belu Spring Water: a new brand of bottled water which is sold in shops and restaurants, but reinvests 100% of its profits in clean water projects in the UK and around the world.

Why they're here...

Sustainability is a key component of a successful social enterprise because it can offer long-term security to its beneficiaries. We're inspired by how Reed and Marilyn cracked this issue by selling the public something they actually want rather than simply asking them to donate cash. belu now sits proudly on the supermarket shelf alongside some of the most commercially driven brands on the market.

?WHAT IF! UnLtd*

Who is Reed Paget?

Reed was born in Seattle in 1968. He studied film in Chicago, then went on to make an award-winning documentary movie, Amerikan Passport, in which he toured global trouble spots of the late 1980s. He's worked in various roles including political merchandising for the 1996 presidential campaign, working as a camera man for Cable One News, and making environmental campaigning films for the UN.

Who is Marilyn Smith?

Marilyn was born and brought up in California and her business career started aged 14 at the Hollywood Farmers market. She studied Theology, Psychology and Business at college before going on to work for Tokai Financial Services, GE Capital and Paramount Pictures. Having been involved with community action groups since childhood her social conscience finally got the better of her in 2002 when she left big business to join Reed and belu.

The issues they confronted

- One quarter of people on Earth don't have access to clean water.

- 50% of hospital beds around the world are taken up by people suffering from water-related illnesses.

- London water has been through six toilets before it reaches a glass.

- By 2025 the demand for fresh water is expected to rise 56% beyond the amount actually available.

The solution they created

- belu was launched in 2004 and is now available in the grocery chain Waitrose, several London restaurants and bars, plus commercial and government offices throughout the South East.

- belu is sourced in Shropshire, on the Welsh border.

- belu donated £7,000 in 2004 to clean water projects. It has already invested in the Gawdesy clean water project in Tamil Nadu, India, which provides the local community with clean water, sanitation and hygiene education, and they are going to partner with Thames 21 and the Lea Valley Trust to help clean UK waterways.

- In July 2005 belu launched in the UK's first compostable plastic bottle, which is made from corn! This means it fully returns to the earth (biodegradeable means it just breaks into smaller pieces).

Reed's story

From graffiti to FMCG...

The inspiration behind belu was kind of an evolutionary thing. I've always been motivated by environmental issues: be it chopping down the forests, nuclear pollution or otherwise depleting the planet so we can drive Mercedes. To put it politely, I thought that this reflected 'misplaced values'.

When I was a teenager I expressed my environmental views through graffiti, when I was a bit older it was film making, and most recently this concern for the planet has manifested in a bottled water company working to fund clean water projects.

The step from film to business was inspired by a job I had working with the Global Compact at the UN. This group put the likes of Shell, Nike, and Daimler Chrysler together in a room with Amnesty International, Human Rights Watch and World Wildlife Fund, in order to jump-start a discussion: 'can business be engaged in solving global problems?'. The answer is that although business and NGOs have different agendas, there is much common ground for cooperation.

Whilst considering the possibility of using business to address social and environmental issues, I began asking myself the question rather than sitting on the sidelines as a journalist and pointing fingers at the business community, what if I set up my own company and ran it from an environmentally minded point of view? If successful, there was the potential to improve the environment simply by winning market share.

After considering various products in the grocery store, the idea of launching a brand of bottled water that would fund clean water projects sprung to life.

What really appealed about putting a product in the grocery store was not only the ability to raise capital, but the potential to raise awareness about an incredibly important issue (the fact that one quarter of the people on the planet don't have clean water at all). Much like the 'dolphin safe' tuna logo engaged the public in the plight of dolphins, an eco-friendly bottled water brand might well inspire the public to help look after the planet's water supply.

The first idea was to create a kite mark for water companies and suggest to someone like Evian that they give 5 to 10% of their profits to clean water projects. That's still not a bad idea, and to be honest if Evian took it on it would deliver more cash to clean water projects than belu will for the next few years at least. The problem with that idea however, is that giving 5-10% doesn't present the same authenticity of purpose from the consumer angle. They would look at 5-10% and say, 'yeah but someone's

making the 90%'. The way to get around that view was obvious; give away 100% of our profits.

That realisation gave us a real challenge: on the one hand we had a great story, people would think, 'wow that's kind of cool' because it's an entirely charitable venture with nothing about personal profit; the downside, and still our biggest challenge, is that when you remove the profit element you lose access to most of the sources of capital that generally fund start-up businesses. So we had a great marketing story, and had built a great 'virtuous concept', but we'd also given ourselves one great big Achilles heel; where to find money.

The five big steps to now...

I had a media communications background; I didn't know what a financial model was, a profit and loss statement, a balance sheet, a cash flow statement, I'd never read a business plan, I didn't really know the difference between marketing and advertising, I didn't know anything about sales, price, margin, bottle cap closures or pallet configurations. The list of the thousands of things needed to actually make something happen is pretty bloody daunting.

1: Be creative...

Having no cash meant that we couldn't hire in experts, so if we needed something done, we would read a book, learn how to do it ourselves, and do it ourselves. To my surprise it's been a really creative experience. As a film maker I was very surprised by the creativity involved in traditional business, be it product design to sales, distribution, financing, etc.

2: Be confident...

We also went seeking help and quickly discovered that a bit of confidence and the ability to write a good letter goes a long way. Very early on we went to the third largest bottling company in the world and got to sit across the table from the Managing Director, despite the fact we had virtually nothing; no name, no bottle design, just the basic idea. But they took us very seriously, and said: 'OK come back when you've got your bottle design and we'll do this at x price...'

3: Use free help...

We also found that there were people and organisations out there who simply wanted to make this happen, so we built a small community of supporters and that's been key. Help has come in all forms, from financial advice to label design to office space. We found an innovation company called ?What If! who was working on a similar idea and together we decided that two heads were better than one. We went to the design house Lewis Moberly, with no money, and they agreed to create our packaging design. These are just two of the many who mucked in with belu simply because they wanted to see it happen.

4: Make it real...

The big 'crossing the Rubicon' was actually getting our first bottle out; an 8 to 10 week no sleep challenge. We got listed in the Waitrose grocery chain and were given a delivery date but at the time all we had was a design mock-up; our bottle had never seen a factory. Lots of door knocking hastily followed, a few gracious people saw how much effort we'd already put in, made a judgement that we weren't going to quit, and decided to give us enough capital to start manufacturing.

5: Be prepared to make sacrifices...

The impact of two or three years working seven day weeks is a kind of glazed look permanently fixed on my face. If I worked a normal job for a normal company I would have savings, take holidays, maybe have a house or a car, but working for this company which has never really paid me I don't have any of these things. So, my girlfriend's not entirely pleased, and we don't have a lot of money for nice meals out.

But, the beauty of being an entrepreneur of any description is that technically you could take a vacation anytime you want! However, if you did everything would fall apart, but just having that theoretical freedom is still pretty cool! The plan is that this current phase of no cash and long hours won't last forever, and seriously, if you compare life in London to life in countries without clean water, I feel comparatively blessed.

Time to bring in the experts...

The business is now really starting to scale up so we're bringing in a management team. This is a really interesting moment for us: if we don't hire we run the risk that things start falling through the cracks, but increasing our team also means we suddenly have the responsibility of paying salaries every month.

There are also some real cultural implications when we hire people: the original staff have been working seven day weeks and haven't ever really been paid; new members are willing to work 9 to 5 and want decent sized salaries. But to my mind, if we're going to be successful we can't remain what is essentially a bunch of idealists trying to figure out marketing, distribution, sales and finance. Let's get people in who are good at those things, the cream of the industry, even if it means paying them more than we pay ourselves. We don't need them to pretend to be environmentalists (although ideally they'll come

round to that way of thinking!) we want their sector expertise to combine with our ideals to do the best for belu. And, whoever we hire, the company itself has its core goals and values and these won't change.

All being well...

There might come a time when we want to take belu overseas, and that will probably involve Marilyn or myself going to other countries to replicate the brand. The ideal is to become one of the top one or two brands in this market; we've really emphasised having a quality product that looks and tastes as good as, if not better than its competitors, so all we have to do is get consumers to buy into the values. I genuinely think we can give the existing competition a run for their money.

I'll certainly be with belu on a day-to-day basis for the next few years. Beyond that? I'm very interested in global warming issues, and now I've learnt all these fascinating new business skills, I could see myself starting some kind of energy business which minimises CO_2 emissions.

Marilyn's story

Getting hooked

I spent most of my career working in corporate America, but after a time decided that I simply wasn't being fulfilled. I realised that my life could be lousy with money, and it could be lousy without money, so I might as well be doing something worthwhile. I took a vacation to London and looked Reed up, whom I knew through friends in Seattle. He introduced me to belu spring water, I worked on his business plan, and on the back of that he asked me to stay involved.

I went home and found myself working on belu, and soon I was coming back and forth to the UK. My family were really pleased that I was working on this social enterprise, but were a bit concerned that I'd swap California for London. I reassured them that this would never happen, but a few months and several trips later my sister called me and said: 'You've moved to London.' Without really realising it I'd joined the company full time, and Reed and I went on to grow the business together. Building the relationship was a gradual thing; we wanted to get to know each other, make sure we complimented each other, but it's worked and we're a nice combination.

Back slapper!

In theory working for a social enterprise should be very rewarding; you should be able to wake up in the morning, pat yourself on the back and say: 'I'm a fabulous person. I'm doing such a lot of good in the world'. But the day-to-day reality is that you could be

working for a regular business because as you deal with stock issues and invoice problems and sales calls you forget the bigger picture. I'm really interested in the psychology of business and charity and what makes people tick in those worlds. I think you never step away from your ego and at the end of the day you want to matter. You do it for yourself. I'm doing it for myself; it's selfishness, but of the most positive kind! But I still need reminding of why I'm here and not still in a US financial services firm, so I'm heading to India, to Tamil Nadu to see the belu project there. I want to see those lives that have been changed, and remind myself what it's all about.

What's great

I've always loved business, I love the idea of winning, I love to be competitive and all of that, and belu is thrilling because it adds an extra dimension to all that stuff, it bucks the system. We've created a business hybrid that acts as a business engine to create a charity annuity for social change. We trick the system by giving away all our profits, and that gives us a real edge over the rest of the market. If I made calls about launching a regular water business chances are people would say 'You and a hundred others honey, see you in a couple of years'. When you tell them about this concept where if they take our water they get the same benefits as with any other supplier and at the same price, but they get to tell their customers a great story, suddenly they stay on the line.

A business like belu also gives us permission to call pretty much anyone in town because we have an agenda beyond personal gain. We've got great relationships with people like John Bird, Anita and Gordon Roddick, and we got to go backstage at Live 8! Recently I was sitting between Water Aid and Clifford Chance, two of the world's biggest organisations in their respective fields, and belu is sitting in the middle having brought them together; I mean how often does that happen?

Taking the plunge

A few weeks ago we went from treading water and searching for funding to getting on the phone and selling. I think that was the moment we actually started to believe we could earn enough from sales to make this business fly. We called bars, restaurants, hotels… and word started to get around. Suddenly we're far from treading water, and the 'push-pull' thing has flipped around so people are calling us. We're making sales and we're attracting new investors, and for the first time it's not those people who specifically support social enterprise, we're now able to stake an investment claim from the mainstream, risk averse organisations.

Looking forward

To say we haven't considered being on a par with Evian would be an absolute lie; of course we've fantasised about being global and having the public see belu as a viable, regular business. Originally I thought that after six months we'd be ready for me to head back to the States and launch belu there; how naïve! I'd still love to do that, and I'd love to join our foundation and visit the projects belu supports, but I've learnt not to plan with too much detail and that there's a natural flow to how this should develop; it's an organic thing and perhaps we shouldn't dictate too much. I know that I'll never go back to the corporate sector, I'm too excited by the business model we've got with belu. I might not get a share of the profits, but then I never did anyway so what's the difference? At least with belu you get the bragging rights!

Our top tips

"To be honest we think a for-profit social enterprise model is the best way to go. Removing most of the financial incentives that exist for employees and investors makes life very difficult. We only did it because of the connection between the purity of water and the completeness of '100% non-profit'; consumers 'get it'."

"For other ventures I would suggest making really good products in an environmentally friendly manner, then simply beat up the competition who doesn't. Ultimately, if you invent a way to run a car on something other than gasoline, you're doing great; stripping away profit as well just makes it harder to achieve the real goal."

Our call to arms

"If Bill Gates is reading this book we need a couple of million pounds. For everyone else, we need you to go to your local store (if you're buying bottled water), and buy belu."

"If you want to be more proactive, go to your store owner, Mr Tesco or Mr Sainsbury, and if they're not stocking belu suggest that they should."

Ideas you can steal

Be competitive as well as ethical

Many (not all) ethical purchases leave the consumer making a sacrifice either on quality or price; belu's offer is 'as good as your current brand, but with a powerful story'. We think this principle of 'everything else being equal' is the key way to increase ethical production and ethical consumerism.

Make it tangible

The proposition behind belu is incredibly simple and consumers get it: 'you drink, they drink'. And because it's a water product being used to combat a water issue, there is a very tangible sense of the ultimate benefit. We think that where possible, this is the most effective way to market an ethical product.

Create a team spirit

If you have a story as good as belu, people will want to be a part of it. Because Reed and Marilyn are willing to share the credit in the belu story they have managed to pull together a group of people from some of the world's leading companies to support the project. Plus, this collaborative spirit serves to create a brand story of great people getting behind a great project.

Eric Samuels

Community Food Enterprise (CFE): aims to improve health in the London Borough of Newham by selling fresh fruit and vegetables at affordable prices, and engaging local people in health and regeneration issues.

Why he's here...

We think Eric epitomises the 'just do it' attitude of a social entrepreneur; when he discovered that there was no access to fruit and vegetables on his housing estate he went and bought £150 worth of produce and sold it from a disused flat. Today, his social food outlets are based in community centres and schools across his borough and sell fresh fruit and vegetables at cost price to local people. Even more outstanding is that from such humble beginnings, Eric has become a leading figure in food access policy in Britain. Although well supported locally, he still receives no central government funding.

?WHAT*IF!* UnLtd*

Who is Eric?

- Eric was born in 1959 in St Vincent, in the Caribbean; his family moved to Britain in 1966 and settled in St Albans where Eric grew up.

- A committed Christian, he has a degree in Electronics and a diploma in Bible Studies from the USA, where he studied for four years.

- After a long career in banking, Eric set up Community Food Enterprise in 1998; in 2001 he was voted UK Volunteer of the Year, after which he started paying himself a wage. The following year he was elected onto the board of West Ham and Plaistow New Deal for Communities and addressed the Labour Party Conference at Blackpool. He's now the Chief Executive of Community Food Enterprise.

The issue he confronted

- Newham is one of the poorest boroughs in the UK and Cranberry Lane Estate is one of the most densely populated areas in Newham for children under 10 years old. Many families don't have easy access to fresh fruit and vegetables at affordable prices and/or aren't fully aware of the importance of a healthy, balanced diet.

The solution he created

- Community Food Enterprise helps reduce food poverty in the borough by improving access to and availability of health enhancing produce. It also encourages the community to play an active role in health and regeneration issues in Newham; by getting local people involved it's tackling the problem from its root and giving the residents of Newham a say in how things are run.

- The project delivers social benefits by providing schools and local residents with food co-ops, running a fruit delivery scheme aimed at 4 to 6 year olds and operating mobile food shops throughout Newham. It also runs income generating initiatives such as the National Training Programme for Community Food Workers, which Eric helped develop and which is the first programme of its kind in the country.

Eric's story

A happy life in Hertfordshire

I was born on St Vincent, the most beautiful island in the world from what I remember of it. I came to England when I was seven and was brought up in another beautiful place, St Albans.

When I was young I was an athlete. I used to play football for Luton Youth. I used to love boxing and many gyms around the country probably still remember me from my boxing days. I had trials in 1976/77 - about the same time as Ricky Hill was around - and when I didn't make the grade it broke my heart.

I started off working in computers but in the early eighties I moved into banking – where I stayed for 15 years. I was involved a lot with Africa, that was the part of the world I used to specialise in. I lived and worked in Ghana for a while, poverty wasn't something I'd never seen before. Even living there I never got used to it though - I was still moved every day.

Belief and self-belief

I had been a Buddhist since 1980 and in the nineties I converted to Christianity. My family are all strong believers. My mother had always been a Christian and up until the age of 15 I used to go to church every Sunday. It was part of the culture and I had no choice until I was 15 and started rebelling. One of the problems was that no one could answer my questions and so I turned to Buddhism. The difference between the two is that Christians will try to feed you, so they'll give you your bread every day, but Buddhism will give you the seed and a bit of land and show you how to cultivate it. Christians make you depend on them – I believe it goes back to the days of the Empire when Christianity was a form of control – but that's not what Christianity means to me.

In terms of CFE I believe I am planting the seed. I believe absolutely in the empowering of people, and as it's got bigger we put our effort into transferring our skills to others.

It's true I had a banking background which helped. You understand how the market works, how finance works, but what really gave me the edge was the drive to succeed. I really believed in what I was doing and that gave me the drive. If one door closes in Newham, I'll go to the next one. There's always another door, it's just knowing where to go next. And you've got to believe in yourself. I went to Newham Borough Council and got turned down because of one powerful councillor who just said 'It'll never work'. Look at it today.

Welcome to the East Side

In the late nineties my mother was taken ill and in 1998 came to convalesce in Newham, where I have sisters. I used to come and visit her and while I was spending time here I decided to do some research on a dissertation I was doing on poverty for a Theology course. I didn't have a very good knowledge of the borough and when I went out into the wider area I was shocked. I didn't know Newham was one of the poorest boroughs in the country. I used to drive down on the North Circular (from St Albans) to my sister's and it was like a different world. Don't get me wrong, from 1998 to the present day the council have done wonders but back then I found it hard to believe that this level of poverty could exist in England.

My mother got worse and was taken to Newham General Hospital where she later died. For some reason I decided to stay - I wanted to finish off my dissertation – and I lived at my sister's. I was moved by my findings to do something about what I saw. I abandoned St Albans.

It was very difficult at first. Go to a bus stop in St Albans and people queue up, in Newham they knock you out of the way. Also, I had never been involved in any sort of social project or community work before – banking is all about money and 'me-ism'. God, the transformation - it was very difficult.

The idea originally came through the research for the dissertation - it just occurred to me. I had got a house on Cranberry Lane Estate where there are a lot of social issues. It's a horrible place to live if you haven't got a car. In 1998 there were no shops on the estate and there was one way in and one way out. It's a mix of social and private landlords. A lot of asylum seekers live there. I knew from the needs assessment I had done that residents wanted a shop, which was clearly not sustainable. I then came up with the idea of a mobile store, which would sell everything, but when I had done the costing it was obviously going to take a lot of money. It was easier to start with a co-op stall. The very first project in the borough was set up there for Cranberry Lane residents.

Do-it-yourself

I originally went to Newham Council with my proposal and every one just shut the door in my face. Initially, to get the project off the ground I used my own funds. There's no bitterness there at all though – everyone has moved on and to be fair to the council they are our partners now so it's worked out.

So I went to Spitalfields market with £150 of my own money in my pocket to buy produce. I was lucky to have the support of East Thames who were one of the major landlords on the estate. They helped with printing and they gave us an empty flat which we could use as the venue for the first co-op. Then we just publicised it by knocking on doors and leafleting the estate. It was only held once a week for literally an hour.

Because of the ethnic diversity in Cranberry Lane people wanted to get their own foods. Ethnic produce in shops is very expensive, and although we have Green Street market in Newham, which is a mainly ethnic market,

there's problems getting there. God knows how many buses you need to take to get to Green Street. Also, despite the diversity in the borough there is still racism in Newham and lot of people travelling from Cranberry Lane to Green Street risk being abused racially. So people prefer the produce to be brought to them where they can access it safely.

Cranberry Lane was a real success. Literally everyone on the estate would use it. Then what happened was that people outside the estate heard about it and would come down as well. It led to problems with people coming in early from outside and buying up all the produce and leaving nothing for residents when they came in.

We needed to expand. It took two years to make the next step, which although frustrating was good for me as I was on a steep learning curve. I don't do politics now, but I learnt my politics at Cranberry Lane. It was probably a good thing that I had the chance to learn those things there before we expanded.

At the time there were two big new projects; the West Ham and Plaistow New Deal for Communities which had just been funded with £55m of central government money, and the Health Action Zone, both of which one would have thought existed to support projects like this. They're on board now but back then it was different; they both turned me down which didn't exactly make things easy.

Take-off

I then applied to the Millennium Commission, the provider being the King's Fund. This time I was successful in my bid. It enabled me to open two new co-ops in schools and was really the catalyst to what is happening here today. When we started doing co-ops in schools it was unheard of, but is now replicated all over the country. We can deliver fresh produce to the mums as they come to collect their kids — it works really well.

However I must say the money was only one part of it. The Millennium Award also provided training in executing the project and I think this was the best thing I ever did. The skills I learned from that course, they are what transformed me. The course was "Building Healthier Communities" which in fact is now the strap-line we use on our own website. It taught me about community work and politics. It armed me to go out there and do the work.

The real turning point for CFE came in 2001 when I was voted UK Volunteer of the Year. At the time it didn't hit home but it really did make the difference. The Guardian did a fantastic article, even today people still call me referring to that article, and I met Princess Michael who was really interested in the project and the work I was doing. It was mind-blowing. It was a one man band up until that time and then you're invited to Downing Street and ministers are referring to you in speeches. Amazing things happened to me like addressing the Labour Party conference in 2002, appearing on TV, etc. Also since then the project has won numerous awards.

Where we are today

The partnerships I have made since then have been very important. UnLtd was the first in 2001 and has been magnificent, because up until it gave me a small grant I had been working on this unpaid for several years and just relying on my savings from my days in banking. They also helped put the business plan together, which is now the model plan that other food access projects use. Then West Ham and Plaistow New Deal for Communities came on board in 2003 and Tate&Lyle in 2004.

We have farmers' markets in schools now and people come from all over the country to give talks once a month. I'm so pleased that food projects as well as co-ops are now in schools across the borough.

Apples and bananas are the biggest sellers because we do boxes and boxes of them for schools. Ethnic food is huge also. Yams — goodness me if you want to see some of the best fights ever they'll be at the co-op over yams. You always get the best stories out of yams; unfortunately you also get profiteering as well, people coming and buying them up and taking them to the markets. A box can go from £12 to £50.

It's a business, stupid

We set our prices at cost plus 15%, and that 15% is still at least 40% cheaper than supermarkets, sometimes 100% cheaper depending on the produce. And we make sure that despite the fact that it's affordable it is best quality. We have our own buyer at Spitalfields and fantastic relationships with specific suppliers now after all these years. It's about quality and price going hand in glove.

This is a social business. We are not giving food away. Our turnover is over £500,000 of which £200,000 is from our trading activities. Areas of the business can be very "profitable" for want of a better word. CFE is made up of eight different units. For example the Service Delivery Unit, which provides training and consultancy for professional organisations and makes proper money, a large surplus of which goes into other areas, such as Social Food Outlet or Schools Education which will always run at a loss. The principle is, if you can afford it you will be charged the going rate. In 2003/2004 we made a £35,000 surplus, in 04/05 we made a £40,000 surplus. And something that gives me satisfaction is that we pay money back to the exchequer - £6,000 in 03/04 – money that we give back to the country.

We also have these relationships with local businesses that enable them to give something back to their community in a highly visible way. The best example is Tate&Lyle who have provided us with free office and warehousing space (next to their plant in Silvertown) and have their name emblazoned on all our vehicles and publicity.

Our board reflects this business, community and professional mix also: We have the financial director of Tate&Lyle and the managing director of Morgan Stanley sitting on the board, yet the chair is occupied by a local – it's important the project remains led by the community.

We now have 12 employees and some 50 volunteers. It is the largest community food project in the country.

The future

The new challenge is running the National Training Programme for Community Food Workers. We had a fantastic launch at the House of Commons but it's like starting all over again. It's the most innovative course that has ever been designed for community food work and it's going out to the whole country - something that should have been done by the Department of Health or health professionals. But we have done it, I have led that and I'm still trying to get funding from the statutory body, the Department for Education and Skills. So no central funding, yet we're used by the government as an example of best practice, I get invited to Downing Street twice a year, numerous MPs come and visit, etc. You think... well I won't use the word. You have to choose your words sometimes, you have to be disciplined, politically.

The focus is the educational side in the future. The government programme can only do so much, and more needs to be done in educating people. The National Training Programme is also about getting people into work. It consists of seven units, one of which is called Social Enterprise and explains how not only to set up a project, but also how to sustain it. The Programme is accredited by the National Open College Network and there are links with the University of East London where people can take their credits from our course into higher education. We worked in

what is allegedly the worst school in London with 10 of their boys, of whom eight are sitting the National Training Programme in September and will graduate with at least level 1 because of the practical work they have done already. These boys were expected to be failures, leave school with nothing and end up in jail. If just one of them could go on to university at the end, wouldn't it be joyful? I think the National Training Programme is going to be here to stay and we're in talks to make it a degree level programme with East London University.

Love thy neighbour

I love Newham, I love the people and as I travel around on buses I'm known. It was the fourth poorest borough in the country in 1998. Cranberry Lane has the highest concentration of under-7s in the borough, and Newham has the highest proportion of young people in the country. It's a fertile place! Newham was of course the first borough to be classed at the census as 'majority ethnic' – I believe it's 63%. It's the most diverse place in Europe, with 144 different languages being spoken. Some schools have 50 different languages in them.

One of the problems is that for years and years the money has been coming in - Newham has probably had more regeneration money than anywhere else in the country since 1964 - but all the agencies bring in workers from outside the borough and they will be trying to tell people what is good for them. CFE is probably the first agency to work with local people and find out what they want.

I don't mind going in and standing up to the council. I don't like to get into politics but when Newham has for years had 60 councillors all from the same party…that's some democracy. I don't get involved in politics - what I do get involved in is people.

My message

To any aspiring social entrepreneurs I'd say, once you have an idea, go and research it thoroughly. Once you've done the research get a good business plan together; there are great organisations out there who can help you do that.

But what you really need to help you approach funders and open doors is a mentor. I have some fantastic mentors who I can go to and bounce ideas off and that's what you need; before you do something have someone you can brainstorm with. That's what gives you the cutting edge and that's why CFE has done so well, because we have the right people around us and that does make a massive, massive, massive difference.

Michael Norton, a great social entrepreneur, is someone who has had a huge influence on me. I met him when he judged me for the BURA Award and he was instrumental on getting me on to this or that board, saying they needed a practitioner, someone from the community. I think he may have had a part in my Volunteer of the Year award as well – he was certainly on the panel. Today he's like my mentor. I can go to him with problems.

How not to get bitter

I do get aggrieved that we are doing preventative work but we don't get funded by any statutory body. It shouldn't be up to us to do it. The government should be doing it but they don't so we do it. A lot of people think we do get central government funding but we don't, even though we're now running a national programme. The BBC was

following up a White Paper on health and did their story down here (using the vans as a backdrop) so again the government looks good because they are seen to be close to us, but they don't give us any money. The sponsors were pleased though – their names were all over the telly. Locally as well there's no money or assistance from the primary health care trust or the council but if you go there they'll be forever taking credit for the work that we're doing and implying it's their project.

But at the end of the day as long as you're serving the community that's the main thing. It's not about personalities. I'm not going to be here forever – there are other things I want to do outside this project – but for me it would be fantastic if in 20 years time CFE is still here. It's about creating a legacy and knowing that when you walk away and let go it can stand on its own two feet.

The legacy

I like to think the legacy we have left with CFE a lot of people have followed and will follow.

If anyone asks me 'What has been your contribution to Newham?', I reply 'empowerment – meaningful empowerment – of people'. What I personally try to tell people is 'this is your community, you should be telling people what you want, not them telling you what they want'. That's the thing I'd really like to take the credit for.

I also hope the co-ordinated approach will be seen as something I left. When I got here what was available on one side of the borough was inaccessible on the other. That's why I set up Newham Food Access Partnership so everyone who was interested could get round a table, come up with a plan and stop the damn wastage. The duplication in this borough had to be seen to be believed.

Finally

I still haven't finished my dissertation. This project has just taken over my whole damn life.

Ideas you can steal

Keep knocking

Eric spoke of his ongoing frustration at having doors closed on him. Where he should have rightfully expected funding and support he hasn't always found it, but he's kept on knocking. We think that all social entrepreneurs will experience this kind of frustration, whether you're asking for a better recycling pick-up service or applying for thousands of pounds to start a venture. Like Eric, be driven and be thick skinned; a door will open soon, but you might need to bruise a few knuckles along the way.

Live the problem

Through a combination of situations Eric found himself living among, and understanding the needs of, the people of Newham. OK, so it's not always possible to live the lives of those you want to help, but you should make every effort to understand exactly what the issues are and what people need before you start providing a service. Set aside time to really find things out; that sounds obvious, but we're talking about a depth of understanding like Eric had. You might challenge yourself to find out ten new things about your issue when you thought you knew all there was to know. Although it cost him his shoes, a big part of Eric's success was down to the time he spent walking the streets of Newham.

Just do it

Our favourite part of Eric's story comes when, having extensively studied the needs of Newham and really getting to understand the complexities of poverty in the borough, he spent £150 on produce at a wholesale market and sold it on to the local residents at cost. How simple, and how proactive. Eric had proved his point; there was a need and there was a solution. If you too can find a way to articulate your challenge in a similarly powerful way, you really will capture people's attention.

Stay local

Over the last 40 years money has poured into Newham from many different outside sources, but without much input from local people about how it's spent; perhaps unsurprisingly the investment has delivered little. Involving the community that you are trying to help will make sure your project responds to their needs accurately, it will encourage people to understand and engage with it. Where possible it's always good to 'keep it local'.

Jamie Oliver

The Fifteen Foundation: trains unemployed youngsters every year to become top chefs and provides a start to their careers in the Foundation's non-profit restaurant.

Jamie's School Dinners: a campaign to transform school dinners, starting in a London secondary school; the campaign then rolled out to a whole London borough, before successfully lobbying the government to invest in lasting reform.

Why he's here...

Through his Fifteen Foundation Jamie created an exemplary social enterprise, and by televising the process he made the concept of social entrepreneurship accessible to the masses. His School Dinners campaign marked him out as a serial social entrepreneur, and perhaps the most impactful in the UK. For the second time in his career he simply 'got on and did something' about an issue, and the result was two fold: a government committed to one of the largest unplanned expenditures in history, and a nation that experienced being rallied behind a single issue with unprecedented unity.

?WHAT IF! UnLtd *

Who is Jamie Oliver?

Jamie was born in Essex in 1975. His dad runs a pub restaurant so by the time he was eight years old he was peeling potatoes in the kitchens, and by 16 he had left school to pursue his dream of becoming a chef.

After catering college he worked in France, then started his career in London. He was spotted by film crew in 1997 whilst working in the River Café restaurant, and went on to produce three hit TV series as the Naked Chef and several best selling recipe books. In 2000 he became the face of Sainsbury's supermarkets.

Jamie was awarded an MBE in 2003 after the success of the Fifteen Foundation. He is married to Jools and has two daughters; Poppy and Daisy.

The issues he confronted

More than 1 million under 25s in the UK are not in education, employment or training; that's 16% of this age group. Each year more than 5% of all 16 year olds, and 56% of those in care, leave school without any qualifications. 32% of disadvantaged youngsters feel that there was a lack of careers advice in their local community, whilst Britain has one of the world's highest rates of youth suicide and the highest teenage pregnancy rate in Western Europe.

In 1988 compulsory competitive tendering was introduced meaning that school dinner contracts had to be open to commercial companies, but no minimum standards were put in place. School meals are now a business worth £1b per year, but only 35p is spent on average per child's plate. 15% of all under 11s in the UK are classified obese, a rise of 50% in the last seven years. £6b per year is spent on obesity, £3b on diet related issues, and £8b on heart disease, whilst the 110,000 dinner ladies in the UK are paid an average of £82 a week. There is also growing scientific evidence to suggest that junk food has a negative effect on behaviour and a child's ability to learn.

The solutions he created

The Fifteen Foundation is now on its fourth intake of trainee chefs, the restaurant is one of the busiest and most acclaimed in the UK, and it is famous for being staffed by 'excluded' youngsters. There is now a Fifteen in Amsterdam and another soon to open in Cornwall.

On the 16th March 2005 the final episode of Jamie's School Dinners was watched by 5 million viewers. On 30th March Jamie delivered 271,677 signatures for his Feed Me Better campaign to 10 Downing Street. On 13th April the government announced it was to invest £280m to improve school meals; it will be used to: establish a minimum spend of 50p per head for primary school kids and 60p per head for secondary kids; the introduction of nutritional standards; the foundation of the School Meals Trust; training for dinner ladies; Ofsted (the school inspectors) to assess school meal standards; and money for improving cooking facilities in schools.

Fifteen Foundation story

The idea

When we first moved to London, about eight years before the project started, I had a conversation with one of Jools's best friends who was working with 'problem kids'. She explained how they were very erratic and quite aggressive, and the only time they'd really shine, the only time their behaviour improved was when they were taking apart a scooter or cooking. They loved the cooking because they could eat what they made. It was from that point on that I decided I wanted to teach disadvantaged kids to cook.

At first it was just a little dream really, but as things worked out for me in my job, and I realised how lucky I'd been, I resolved to make that dream happen. I would make top chefs out of unemployed young Londoners who had never cooked before. And I'd build a non-profit restaurant where my trainees would cook. Looking back I couldn't have done certain things more wrong, in fact I think I did everything wrong and basically created a monster! But Fifteen is something that I committed myself to, and that I am still committed to, and I put myself on the line because it's bloody exciting and it's totally inspiring.

Fears

From the outset I had loads of worries. Above all I felt totally vulnerable because I was letting fifteen complete strangers into my life. I was going to see more of them than I would my missus, and they might have turned out to be horrible! I also worried about building the restaurant, finding the money, making time in my diary, keeping the missus happy, having a baby, how the public would judge me, the kids not wanting to learn, the kids giving up, the kids just wanting to be part of the fame thing rather than becoming chefs. I don't think any bookie would have taken bets on us pulling this off, and I knew that it really could break me.

A bit Pop Idol

I first got to meet the kids when we had the sessions to take it down from 60, to 30, and then down to the last 15. We devised a few kitchen tests for them, and because none of them were formally trained, and they were all well nervous at the prospect of being back in unemployment, all we really hoped for was a bit of enthusiasm and passion for food. But shit, these guys were completely cold to cooking. They were probably less clued up than your average TV-watching foodie and I wasn't sure why some of them had even turned up. We're talking a real lack of basic knowledge and that scared the life out of me. Having expected it to be really tough to turn away loads of great candidates, the biggest problem was finding 15 we could actually work with.

At the end we did this kind of 'Pop Idol' selection when we had to get rid of some of them and that was pretty rough. The crap thing was that we had to upset these guys that had actually done incredibly well to make it down from the initial 1000. We invited them to come back the following year and we pointed them in the direction of other courses, but that is one of the downsides of Fifteen; what to do with the 985 youngsters that get themselves together enough to apply but don't make it.

Bit of a short sharp shock

To give 'the chosen ones' a kick start we employed a German chef called Herr Bosse, who was a real task master. I remember on the first day he said only six of the fifteen could be 'let loose' in a kitchen. Then we had my old teacher Peter Richards; a chef from the real old school. These guys brought the reality to the students that this was now a course – it wasn't just a selection day with Jamie. We began to see them under pressure; we had ones who pissed around, ones who didn't show up, problems with dyslexia, problems with ADHD (Attention Deficit Hyperactivity Disorder), even problems with violence. Some of the issues were self-inflicted, some were just a result of what happens when you recruit disadvantaged youngsters.

Some of the students turned up to less than 50% of their college days which, to be honest, I just found offensive. One time, I called one of them up to find out where they were and they were in the shopping centre – not with their mates, but with their mum! The mum then got on the phone to me to say how proud she was, but the fact is, she had taken her kid shopping whilst they were supposed to be in class.

The problem for me with all these discipline issues was that I'd committed to take on a bunch of guys with some serious problems, and when the shit hit the fan I really didn't know what to do for the best. I had to think of the long-term impact if we kicked them off the course; some of them already thought of themselves as failures and now we might go and tell them: 'Yep, you're still a failure'. Half of the things that were going on wouldn't have been allowed to happen in the trade, and this was always about training unemployed people to a really professional level and making them employable. I wouldn't be doing them any favours by giving them an easy ride. In any case it was me who would initially be employing these people; they would be representing our restaurant, making starters, cooking pastas, baking breads, doing night shifts. Everything would be scrutinised by the food critics and the press would have their knives out. Balancing our commitment to the students was bloody challenging.

Reality check

After four months of the programme it was time for the students' NVQ Level 1 test. Without it no one in the industry, not even I, could employ them, but over half of them failed. To put this into context, I wasn't very good at school but I found NVQ Level 1 a pretty basic, easy exam. At that stage I felt less than great that all our plans rested with this group of kids

Getting them ready

After the assessments we took them to Cumbria to visit the farm that would be supplying our meat, so that they'd get a feel for where food actually comes from. For some it was their first trip to the countryside, which was great, we even got them mucking out which they hadn't done much of in Hackney!

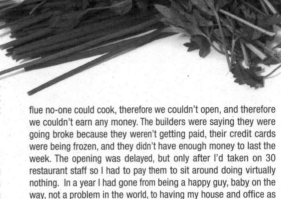

Then it was time to send the students on work experience, and they were given placements at some of the UK's top restaurants. Two of them did a medium rare chicken breast on their first day, luckily not for public consumption or they might have killed someone. It was interesting to see how they responded when the cameras were away and when I wasn't there. It had suddenly become a job. What frightened me was that even with the ones that did well, their chefs would say: 'Yeah I'd keep them, but I wouldn't have 15 of them.' One dropped out on day two, and a couple just took the piss, and then I'd get a call from their chef taking the piss out of me; thinking I was a wanker for having faith in these guys. Some of these head chefs thought the whole charity concept of Fifteen was a load of bollocks, and they told me they wouldn't take any future students.

After work experience I thought the students needed a little test, so I tricked them into thinking they were catering for a party. Luckily it was a mock-up because everything that could go wrong did go wrong. We had bust ups, people were stressing; it was a nightmare and it made me realise how far we were from being ready. I also realised that until now some of them still hadn't grasped the reality of it all: 'I'm a chef'; 'I work down the River Café'; 'We go up to Cumbria to see the lovely pigs and it's all lovely'. I had a £1.8m restaurant for these guys to work in, and it looked like A A Gill was going to be served a dried up bit of old pasta. It was certainly not all lovely. They were rubbish that night, and again it scared the life out of me.

Giving them my reality

That year was bloody stressful, and every day I felt like I might go broke. Initially I went in for 400 grand along with a bit of help from the London Development Agency, but as the months went by I was committing more and more money, then more and more money. People would never come and say: 'Now Jamie it's gone up by 50 quid, just to let you know'; my accountant was having these conversations with me where the costs were going up by 250 grand. Eventually the total went up to £1.8m! I remember in Cumbria one of the trainees let slip that there was a bit of a cynicism in the group: 'Jamie what is this? Is it one big press thing?' So, I told them what it was: 'You haven't seen half of what I've had to go through to make this work. The money has gone up and up. We essentially borrowed the money from the bank, and the bank never just gives you money, especially on that scale. So they've been round my house with a clip board and said 'Right your house is worth this, and your office is worth that, and if this business goes tits up then we'll have them'. And I had to sign underneath saying 'Yeah, course you can'. So, I'm basically in the shit if this doesn't work. So that's what it means to me, and I think at the end of the day that's pretty deep.' The good thing about this little rant was that I think it actually helped them to know this project was proving hard for someone other than them. It was certainly good for me to get it off my chest!

The final push

Shortly before the opening of the restaurant I couldn't really feel any worse. Costs had spiralled out of control, I had 13 inexperienced chefs to run my restaurant (we'd lost two), and we hadn't got any gas because the flue couldn't be fitted. Without a

flue no-one could cook, therefore we couldn't open, and therefore we couldn't earn any money. The builders were saying they were going broke because they weren't getting paid, their credit cards were being frozen, and they didn't have enough money to last the week. The opening was delayed, but only after I'd taken on 30 restaurant staff so I had to pay them to sit around doing virtually nothing. In a year I had gone from being a happy guy, baby on the way, not a problem in the world, to having my house and office as a quarantee and having a bloody mortgage for something I'm never ever going to make a penny from.

With the delay we had to keep the trainees focused so we devised their biggest challenge yet: a charity night at Babington House in Somerset. Although one of the students forgot to powder the trays so all the chocolate tarts stuck, it all went well. We served some great food to 200 people that night and, finally, I felt a lot better about the prospects for Fifteen.

When we did finally open, the kitchen had a huge leak and, with just four hours to go until service, we had builders crawling all over the place and toolboxes everywhere. But, as if by magic the first night happened, and it was great.

The challenge continues

Right from the off we were taking 5,000 calls a day for tables. Despite this, when I sat down with my accountant six months in, expecting to hear about all the profit we were making to pay off the debts, he told me that we were only breaking even. We were working all those hours, and basically not making a penny. A lot of refinements and touching up had been needed and that had just kept eating up all the cash. The toilets alone, fitting them, fixing them, and closing when they broke down cost over £100k!

After about a year things still weren't great. Of the 15 original students we only had eight left, and that was like torture; the whole reason I started this thing was to train unemployed youngsters, and half of them were gone. Of the eight, only three of them were operating properly. Instead of being surrounded by new chefs, I had doctors' notes coming out of my ears. I told them that I didn't spend £1.8m quid to open a restaurant with no-one in it. When I looked around the kitchen and saw no-one there apart from the employed staff it broke my heart.

It was at this time that we started looking for the next intake. I was feeling really aware that other kids might have made a better fist of the opportunity than the seven who'd dropped out, so our big aim was to pick people more likely to last the course. We used one of those adventure weekends in Wales where they would have to spend two days together doing various challenges. I was set on one thing: I didn't want to end up with ten. I wanted to finish the next year with a full complement.

Taking stock

Despite all the shit, we still had some phenomenal results including chefs graduating to work in California, Tuscany and three in Sydney. One event that summed up the great stuff for me was when we got the chance to cook at 10 Downing Street. Although one of the students nipped off for a fag, all I could think about was that a year ago these guys were unemployed… yet now here they were meeting the Prime Minister as chefs!

I know people say how lucky the kids were but I had an amazing experience as well. All my other TV projects just showed everything going smoothly, but I was a chef working at home in my own kitchen so I'm hardly going to blow things up. This was about my day job. It showed how hard I work, how passionate I am, and how I love to teach. I look like shit most of the time and get caught swearing 20 times in the first 30 seconds, but I put myself on the line and in the end just about every student charmed me. Take Kerry-Anne; she messed me around no end at the start of the course, but I knew she'd be a chef one day. One night I got a call from her at 12.45am when I was in bed with Jools. She had this great new idea to spice up one of the desserts and she wanted to tell me about it. I get such a buzz from that kind of enthusiasm. Now, everyday when we're in service, I look down the line in the kitchen and see those that finally made it. I see the elegance in their fingertips as they're making wonderful salads, or beautiful pastas and I see that they're really hungry for it. We can let them go now and they'll go on to do wonderful work, and that's what I'm really proud of.

It'll take about eight years to pay off the debts before we start breaking into profit, but if I had wanted to make my life easy I would have retired. I wanted to do something a bit risky and a bit mad, and I knew that if I'd left it a year or two I would have been a bit too sensible to have done it. It's a lifelong thing, and we had to be able to make mistakes that first time. We take on a new group every year – this year it was 20 – and I know that down the line each of them are going to teach and spend time with their young chefs, like we've taught and spent time with them. And it's nice to have that kind of thing in catering because it's a tough industry, but it's a great industry.

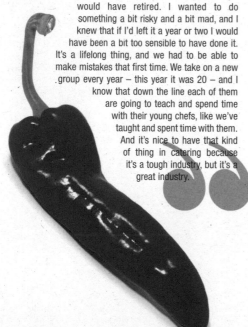

Jamie's School Dinners story

Why school dinners?

I started this project because I wanted British kids to eat better food, I wanted them to be healthier, and I wanted them to grow up with better eating habits. I want us to have a better, cooler, cleverer, healthier nation. School dinners are Britain's greatest public health question, and I was fed up with just saying 'school food's crap' … I wanted to do something about it.

So, I decided to devote a year of my life to totally changing school dinners in one school, then taking control of a borough and getting a whole bunch of schools doing wicked things that we could be proud of. My dream for the end of the year was to annoy the government, and to be able to say: 'Right, listen to us now: we know what we're talking about, this is what we're going to do, and if you don't do it it's because you don't give a shit about our kids.'

I spent that year working in a school in Greenwich and every day I would drive past the Millennium Dome and it fucking haunted me; 800m quid … what I could have done with that money. How can we have got into a situation where we're asking schools to cook growing kids a meal for the price of a packet of crisps? How come I've met loads of 15 year olds who can tell me all about drugs but they don't know what celery or courgettes taste like?

Friends and family couldn't work out why I took this on, but that's because they were going home every night and giving their kids a lovely meal, and that just isn't the norm. My vision was dead simple: it doesn't matter who a kid is, they will get five good meals a week, and they'll get them at school because that's the only way of knowing that they're getting them. And then, just maybe, the surgeries might empty and the classrooms be full of sweet, attentive kids.

What we were up against

In a nutshell, the School Dinners story goes something like this: 20 years ago the government gave up responsibility for school dinners. Ever since, the quality has been going down and down and down, and today it's an absolute shit fight. As a consequence, Britain has all those horrible stats listed earlier, and there are some serious, ingrained barriers to get over if we are to make a change.

Kids are totally ignorant about healthy food. I was in a class of nine year olds and they could name only seven of 50 vegetables. Only one knew what leeks were and one thought an asparagus was a kiwi, but they could all recognise the Domino's Pizza logo.

Kids' tastes are totally closed. Nora, my amazing dinner lady, summed it up: 'You get beautiful children coming into school aged four choosing burger and chips and they leave at 16 doing the same.'

Then there is this myth, successfully peddled by the catering companies, that kids as consumers have the right to choose what they eat. Yet, you don't get parents insisting their kids be allowed to read a comic book in their English class instead of Shakespeare; you don't consider allowing kids the right to smoke; we collectively say 'no' to certain stuff, but not to kids wanting to eat junk food.

Then there are loads of issues with parents, and these are the ones that no government really wants to talk about. Many of the last two generations of parents don't know how to cook so a load

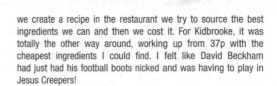

of kids are given cash seven days a week for a KFC, a burger, a portion of chips… More and more parents are working every day so have less time to cook from fresh. Often families will eat in two sittings: chicken nuggets and chips for the kids, then proper food for the adults later. I hate that; why do parents feed their kids stuff that they wouldn't eat themselves? Again it's a new trend inspired by large companies that know fuck-all about food and create these 'meal solutions' for parents: 'Stick it in the freezer; it will last for months and will make your life easier and better.' In reality it's processed crap, the same crap served up in schools, and is marketed to control what our kids eat. I met one entire class of ten year olds who had all had chips the night before except one who'd had a Pot Noodle. All the government has done is encourage this by giving incentives to get mothers back to work, but they do nothing to deal with the consequences.

Everyone's terrified of having a go at parents; I'm a parent, I know we all strive to do our best, but we have to stuff being politically correct and start to criticise people who knowingly feed their kids crap food. A paediatrician in Greenwich told me that if the insides of some kids' bodies were visible to the outside world, their parents would be locked up for child abuse. He told me it was quite normal for kids to throw up shit because they couldn't go to the toilet as they weren't eating any fruit or vegetables. During my year at Kidbrooke School, I found parents handing McDonald's to their kids through the railings, and I had parents coming up to me and saying: 'Oi, are you responsible for that menu? It's crap.' Unfortunately, no government is up for telling parents that they're killing their kids, but they are, and we have to face up to it.

Compare all this to South Africa, where I'd just been for Comic Relief. We found school dinners served in a shanty town that were better than the vast majority of the dinners served in Britain. We have a bloody crisis in this country where, for the first time in history, there is a generation of kids who might die before their parents just because of their diet.

Starting at the bottom

At Kidbrooke there are 1,400 kids. 700 of them qualify for free school meals, and when I got there 500 pupils were choosing to eat in the canteen each day (which means even some of those who were getting food for free were rejecting it). Nora was serving up nasty Botswanan free flow minced beef with a quarter of a tonne of chips a week, accompanied each day by just half a pot of peas. As she put it, 'You could give veg away and still no-one would eat it.'

I started by just mucking in as a dinner lady. On my first morning I laid out pizzas, fish fingers, sausages… most of it was reconstituted, which means you just don't know what's inside it. The girls were running a very tight ship and their attention to detail was great, but the food was shite. That day, every single child who came through that canteen had a totally unacceptable, unbalanced diet. We had it analysed by a nutritionist: there was no fruit and veg, therefore no vitamin C, therefore no immunity, which in turn means more time off school with illness; there was a third of the required amount of iron, therefore kids would find it hard to concentrate and achieve less at school. So, not only was the food I'd just prepared and served to 500 kids seriously unhealthy, but it was actually detrimental to the kids' ability to learn. It was totally irresponsible.

After a week or so I tried to create a healthy dish within the school's budget. However hard I tried, I just couldn't do it. When we create a recipe in the restaurant we try to source the best ingredients we can and then we cost it. For Kidbrooke, it was totally the other way around, working up from 37p with the cheapest ingredients I could find. I felt like David Beckham had just had his football boots nicked and was having to play in Jesus Creepers!

After two weeks I sent Nora off to Fifteen for a day while I ran her school kitchen. I loved the prep, but the food was late out and the junk food was massively more popular than my efforts. I had also spent over a quid a plate rather than 37p which meant the headmistress had to spend funds reserved for books or staffing. The only good news came from Fifteen, where Nora got exposed to a place and a team totally passionate about food. It was like we'd turned a light on in her around food, it was wonderful.

So after stage one of my campaign to persuade the government to transform school meals I had managed to transform one dinner lady, but none of my dishes had come in on budget, the kids were still eating junk, and at home I had a daughter with a temperature of 104. I wasn't getting paid for any of this and it was not going well.

The young ones

Next I went up to County Durham to find out about younger kids. That area had come out statistically as the most unhealthy region in England, which is some label to have. At the school I went to, 70% of the kids qualified for free school meals which were provided by a company called Scolarest. I had lunch on the first day in the canteen; the most intelligent kid there was the one eating a tomato ketchup sandwich.

That night I stayed with a family on the local estate, and they served up Turkey Twizzlers. There's 30% turkey in one of these things, so God only knows what constitutes the other 70%… I asked the family, as an experiment, not to let their kids eat junk food for one week. Incredibly, the kids were instantly more loving and they stopped lashing out after they had eaten; it was how the parents wanted their family to be. At the end of the week they decided to give the kids some cans of pop and tinned spaghetti hoops as a treat; thirty minutes later they were a nightmare and straight back to throwing tantrums. I always knew that food could change a kid's behaviour, but to see such a dramatic change first-hand totally inspired me. If I could get school dinners right, imagine the impact it would have in classrooms.

Hearing what we were up to in one of their schools, Scolarest rang to talk things over. I explained how it was pretty hard not to slate them when they were willingly preparing crap products for kids, some of whom relied on school dinners for half of their daily nutritional intake. They agreed to let me cook a meal for the whole school on the last day of term. I was well nervous that the kids would just throw my food in the bin and the Scolarest girls would sit there laughing at me, but against all our expectations the kids happily tucked in to the most nutritious lunch they'd ever had at school. One lad proudly told me that he'd had five scoops of salad, and it was the first time he'd ever eaten it. The head cook, Mavis, got three cheers from the kids and was in floods of tears. She told us she felt 20 foot tall. The fact that we got all those kids eating that stuff was a sign to any council or major company that says, 'We're just giving them what they want, they'll only eat burgers.' That just wasn't true and I'd proved it. Every kid there had eaten the food and 99% of them had enjoyed and preferred it. I went home that day very, very happy.

Back in London I went to see the Scolarest boss, Tony Sanders – the man with the responsibility for serving almost a million school dinners every day. I wanted him to ban the junk food that the kids were so fond of. I told him that I cooked the meal in Durham on budget, and that I provided fresh fruit, fresh meat, fresh vegetables… I had seven vegetables in our tomato sauce. I told him that Scolarest needed to be the first company to ban all the reconstituted meat products and I asked him to ban Turkey Twizzlers. He said that the kids would vote with their feet if we removed 'recognisable items' off the menu, and then a lot of the children who were entitled to a free meal wouldn't get their food. We didn't get very far.

Time to get tough

When I got back to Kidbrooke it was three weeks since my food had been introduced and we had stacks of complaints from the kids, 80% of whom were still eating the crap. We even had a kid tell the Daily Mail 'Jamie's food tastes disgusting, it's all whippy dippy fancy do'. This is when the dietician told me that some kids were having so much saturated fat that they were throwing up their own faeces! That was it. The softly, softly approach hadn't worked so I decided to totally ban junk food there and then. We didn't tell the kids before we did it. One day they turned up and for the first time in 13 years there was no junk food on the menu.

Nora was so worried she couldn't speak, and she was right to be. The kids totally rejected it. They wanted pizza, they wanted chips, and they wouldn't try anything different. Most of the food we served that day went in the bin. After three days numbers in the canteen had dropped dramatically, and those left made it a battle ground by refusing to clear their plates, and calling me every name under the sun. Now I was worried. Perhaps school dinners was one step too far. I began to wonder whether I was getting cocky; this wasn't a formatted thing, it wasn't just setting up a kitchen. This was almost brainwashing, this was trying to get kids to change their bad habits. I really wasn't sure I could pull this one off.

Looking at the bigger picture

Trying to remain positive I went to see Greenwich Council. The whole thing really hinged on them; there would be nothing newsworthy or profound if we just changed one school, but if we changed an entire borough we could show the government what they needed to do. My only previous experience of councils was trying to get parking tickets removed so I wasn't exactly sure what to expect! I explained my vision to them, and said that I would need access to all their head teachers and head dinner ladies. At the end of the meeting they said they were up for it.

So, I had all the Greenwich head teachers over to Fifteen where I served them exactly what we'd served at Kidbrooke that day. I was really honest about how hard it had been, about the complaining kids and the complaining parents, but almost all signed up there and then and that meant we could roll out in just six weeks' time. It also meant that the consequences of me screwing this up had just gone through the roof! We were about to be responsible for feeding 20,000 kids every day.

After a tour of the school kitchens in Greenwich I realised there was loads to do. The dinner ladies I met represented thousands of kids each, and they didn't even have basic training; they had been reduced to box openers. In my efforts to return them to being cooks I needed Nora's help, so I nicked her out of Kidbrooke for two days a week and together we designed recipes and planned a 'dinner lady boot camp' to get them up to speed as quickly as possible. Going into the camp we got some great news from Kidbrooke; the complaints had just about dried up, numbers in the canteen were back up, and we had kids eating healthy food. Nora had cracked it, and now she was going to tell these other dinner ladies how to do it at their schools.

On a wet Wednesday morning during the October half term, 60 dinner ladies arrived in Aldershot at the army school of catering. They gave up their holiday for an intensive course where, in just three days, they would learn what had taken me six months to teach Nora. They might have boiled the buggery out of their veg, and not had a clue how to cook pasta properly, but when we brought in 400 squaddies for them to feed, they did brilliantly. I left feeling very happy and filled with confidence for the Greenwich takeover. As they left I told them that they were leading probably the most important food revolution that had ever taken place in the UK.

All systems go

Then the roll-out started. Every week five new schools joined the project and if they had any problems they had my number. On the first day we had new equipment not turning up, people stressing, people having to do extra hours, people threatening to leave, kids rejecting it. Suddenly this wasn't just me and Nora going through shit, this was real dinner ladies' lives, their hours, their emotions and their pay cheques being messed around with and it was serious stuff.

To give the schools a bit more support I produced a pack that contained all the recipes, including tips on how to cope in the kitchen, plus how to run what we called a food week where the kids learn about stuff to do with food in every subject (in order to try and help persuade the most stubborn kids to try stuff). A month in and 5000 kids in 25 schools were being fed our dinners, and what was really incredible was that teaching staff were already noticing that the kids were behaving better and could work for longer. Not only that, but one school, who had been handing out asthma pumps on a daily basis, hadn't had to use the pumps once since starting on my meals. Behaviour and health had improved after just one month. If the government ignored this, if they wouldn't now add another 10p to a plate or invest in training dinner ladies then surely that would say they didn't care about our kids at all.

Taking it to the top

By Christmas the dinner ladies of Greenwich had done us proud, but many of them were having to work unpaid overtime to make it work. It was time to go and see the government, so I fixed a meeting with the Secretary of State for Education and Skills, Charles Clarke.

He came down to Fifteen where Nora and I served him the shit that used to be on the school menus, followed by the good stuff that was now being served in Greenwich. We explained that kids, as long as they were given the right to choose, would always go

for the rubbish junk. It went pretty well. He sounded enthusiastic and excited, and everything Nora and I were passionate about he agreed with. Two days later David Blunkett resigned, Charles Clarke was moved to Home Secretary, and Ruth Kelly was appointed the new Education Minister.

After the show had aired on television I managed to arrange a series of meetings with Ruth Kelly and her team at the DfES. Whether what happened was because they really cared, or just because the show created such a storm and there was an upcoming election just a few weeks away, I don't really care, but after much to-ing and fro-ing we really got somewhere. £280m was pledged to set up a trust, train dinner ladies, guarantee 50p a plate, introduce minimum standards, and basically take this thing bloody seriously. It was a long and difficult road and, to be honest, just like with Fifteen, I took something on without having a clue how big it would get and how it would impact on my life. The whole thing snowballed completely out of control but, just like at Fifteen, we saw it through to the finish and I'm over the moon with where we got to.

Ideas you can steal

Stick to what you know

Jamie was a chef who wanted to 'do good', so he staffed his restaurant with disadvantaged youngsters. He didn't try to solve third world debt - he did what he was qualified to do; we think this is how everyone, including companies, should do their bit. Having a group of accountants volunteer to paint school fences is great, but surely their expertise could be used to greater effect elsewhere.

Quality not quantity

The Fifteen Foundation does not solve the issue of youth unemployment. In fact, it has a relatively low impact in terms of statistics. But what it does, it does exceptionally well and therefore provides a model of best practice the world can follow. Not every project can eradicate a social issue, but every project should inform and inspire others to act, and that's a perfectly valid way to achieve scale; do what you do very well and others will replicate your work.

Demonstrate your impact

Jamie wanted to improve school dinners throughout the UK, but before he approached the government he showed it was possible in one school and then one borough. People react when you have already proven your point, but struggle when you talk in proposals and plans; demonstrating your impact is the way forward.

Present your story so people get it

OK so we can't all produce a four part documentary for national TV, but you can be imaginative in how you present your work. The more tangible the better; bring to a meeting those people that will benefit from it, tell real stories, get those you need to influence into the action so that they can't help but engage.

Be an annoying friend

Throughout Jamie's interactions with government he resisted the temptation to stand fully against or alongside them. Sometimes you need to engage with people even when they feel like the enemy, and equally to remain independent even when faced with an attractive ally. Jamie stubbornly and skilfully stuck to the role of annoying friend and that was key to the final result.

Eugenie Harvey

We Are What We Do: a movement which aims to change the world by inspiring as many people as possible to make simple changes in their everyday lives.

Why she's here...

Eugenie has led the development of We Are What We Do into what is fast becoming a worldwide consciousness-raising movement promoting social change and involvement. The basic idea is simple and brilliant: everyone has the power to make a small change to improve things, lots of people making lots of small changes equals social change on a massive scale. Eugenie has been spearheading the movement for which her book, Change the World For a Fiver, provides the funds. As well as the unprecedented scale of the movement, we also think what sets it apart from other initiatives is its tone; Eugenie has proven that you don't need to sound worthy to do good, and that perhaps we'll have a greater chance of changing the world if we do it with a smile.

?WHAT IF! UnLtd*

Who is Eugenie Harvey?

Eugenie was born in Sydney in 1968; she studied Communications at Sydney University of Technology and landed her first job with the Sydney Theatre Company, first as a publicist and then as Public Relations Manager.

She then joined the Murdoch-run TV company, FOXTEL, as Public Relations Manager where she worked for three years.

Eugenie moved to London in 1999 and after a brief attempt at stand-up comedy decided to keep her day job at the financial PR company, Brunswick. Here she had a chance encounter with David Robinson who runs a charity called Community Links. They joined forces to launch We Are What We Do.

In September 2004 she published Change the World For a Fiver which became an instant bestseller.

The issues she confronted

People today are far less likely to be part of clubs, societies or a church. We're less likely to know our neighbours and are more mistrustful of people in the street than ever before. We work harder, live faster and consume more and more, whilst taking less time out to do things for ourselves.

At the same time more people than ever are volunteering for community projects, ethical shopping is on the increase, and the internet has led people to be generally more aware of world issues.

The solution she created

Eugenie launched We Are What We Do in Spring 2004; the website offers simple, everyday ideas to improve the environment, our health and our communities, and invites people to share new ideas for action. The ideas range from visiting a neighbour to recycling your plastic bags. By September 2005, nearly 80,000 people from around the world had pledged to take action.

When Change The World For a Fiver was published in September 2004 it sold 100,000 copies in a hundred days and it's now being launched internationally. A follow-up book, Change the World 9-5 comes out in April 2006; its aim is to take the original concept into the workplace, encouraging people to make simple changes within their everyday working environment.

Eugenie's story

On the outside looking in

I was born in Sydney in Australia in the sixties and for me growing up I always felt an outsider. I come from a very middle class family and had what you'd call quite a protected childhood, I was very lucky, but I never really had a real sense of 'belonging'. I suppose that's partly because of the fact that I was an extremely overweight child and teenager and that affected me quite deeply, it made me feel different.

That feeling of being on the outside continued at university, but my experiences there also gave me a fantastic window into a world that wasn't as rosy as the one I'd grown up in. I did Communications, which was quite a radical degree at that time in Sydney, it was pretty left-wing and was full of people who'd had very different experiences from me, people who for various reasons had been outside the system. That was a real eye-opener and was quite a significant period of my life.

My first proper job was at the Sydney Theatre Company, which is a big arts organisation like the National Theatre over here. I worked in the publicity department and absolutely loved it. After a few years I started to wonder what my next move would be and then saw a job advertised working for Rupert Murdoch as Public Relations Manager. So I applied for the job, got it and spent three years working in a corporate communications role for a great big Murdoch company, from start-up.

It seems strange when I look at where I am now, what I'm doing with We Are What We Do, and compare it to those days of working in a big corporate environment. But I believe that sometimes in order to get to where you want to be, you have to journey as far away from that point as you possibly can. At that time I knew that working in that kind of environment was very far removed from where I wanted to be, but at the same time I didn't know exactly where it was I wanted to be. So I thought to myself, you'd be a fool to let this opportunity pass and I

just put my head down and stuck with it. It was definitely useful in developing certain skills that have stood me in good stead in the work I do now.

But I couldn't shake this feeling of emptiness; I'd got to about 30 and started feeling pretty down about where I'd got to professionally. I also felt a lot of pressure to succeed; Sydney is a small place, especially when you've lived there all your life, and I felt a lot of pressure to go down a certain route and fulfil other people's expectations of me.

Living the dream

That's when I thought I'd give London a try (my dad was born in Wood Green so I've got a British passport). I thought that I'd be freer to try something new and, if I failed, it wouldn't matter as much because no-one knows me.

I had never really had a clear plan of what I wanted to do with my life; I was a reasonably bright girl and obviously had a lot of opportunities, and I expect a lot of people thought I'd go on to become a lawyer or something similar. But I did have one thing I was certain of and that was a real desire to move or affect people in some way. I was always passionate about the performing arts and had a childhood dream of becoming a comedian. My dad's a very funny man; I thought I'd inherited that wit and that I'd be able to pull it off.

So that was my big challenge on arriving in London. By day I worked at the Australian Tourist Commission, which was great fun – we did a lot of work promoting Australia to English journalists in the run up to the Sydney 2000 Olympics – and at night I was going out around town trying to get myself known on the comedy circuit. The one thing I learned during that time is that I wasn't a gifted comedian by any stretch of the imagination!

Ironically, it was kind of a fantastic thing to find that out. Because I think if there's something you've always thought in your heart of hearts you really want to try, it's far better to try it and fail than to always be wondering, 'Could I?' Which isn't to say it's not incredibly galling to discover that you're shite at something you thought you'd be talented at. But in many ways I have absolutely fulfilled the dream I had which in a big way enabled me to move on and think 'what next?'

Reality bites

At the same time, the feeling of not knowing where I was heading, or wanted to be heading, was growing. While I was at Brunswick – which I should add is a fantastic organisation! – it started eating away at me and I got more and more angry at myself because I couldn't work out what this 'thing' was that I was missing. I realise now that

I was experiencing what I think a huge number of people in the western world these days feel, which is a huge sense of isolation, loneliness and emptiness.

It's shocking the extent to which people are feeling the effects of this consumerist society we live in. The fact is, personal consumption, which has risen to phenomenal levels recently, isn't making us happier, it's making us feel more disenfranchised and disillusioned than ever. Satisfaction with life was higher during post-war rationing than it is now.

I started to get pretty depressed. I felt like I hadn't achieved anything and that I was a failure. Just because I wasn't in the gutter and didn't appear to be down and out to other people, didn't mean that I wasn't feeling it myself. What I hadn't appreciated at the time is that 'the outside' is in fact an incredibly crowded place – everyone in the world at some point feels on the outside and everyone feels it in different ways.

To top it all, my sister had her second child at around that time. She rang me up from the hospital bed and said "I've just had another little girl, her name's Poppy" and obviously I was really happy for her but I felt so far away personally from the happiness that she was experiencing that it really felt like the nail in the coffin.

That event in fact turned out to be quite an epiphany for me. The great thing about hitting rock bottom is that there's only one way to go and that's up. So I started to think, hang on, you've got a good education, you've got your health, you've got a family who love you, you've got work experience and skills that you've developed for more than a decade, you don't have the financial obligations that a lot of people have, or personal commitments and I realised that I had the most extraordinary liberty and good fortune – combined with a real desire to do something positive. All of a sudden it was as clear as a bell.

Happy chance

I knew then that I wanted to use this empathy I had for people like myself, who were missing out on all that life has to offer because of unhappiness or lack of fulfilment, to make a difference. And then serendipity stepped in.

David Robinson, who was head of an east London charity called Community Links, came to Brunswick to give a talk about the causes and consequences of community exclusion. What he said really struck a chord. He talked about the paper he'd written, called 'Reconnecting' which examined the power of brand advertising and how it could be used just as validly in the not-for-profit sector to promote community involvement and responsibility. So he had these ideas that were very loosely formed and had also gathered together some people who were keen to take the ideas forward.

Discovering your passion

I knew that finally I could use my skills for something I could really be proud of, something that would galvanise people to take action and help them feel part of something bigger than themselves. So I quit my job and started developing We Are What We Do with David. The challenge for us was to make sure it wasn't a flash in the pan; it had to be sustainable. We used Mahatma Gandhi's idea that "We must be the change we want to see in the world" as a starting point. But we were adamant that we didn't want it to become another voluntary sector, 'holier than thou' thing.

What really drove the project in the early stages – and what still drives it - is passion. I wanted to make a difference, I wanted to do something, I wanted it to work. And that's helped shape my life philosophy over the last three years of doing this project; it's driven into me the belief that each one of us can do something and we have a responsibility to do it.

Keeping the faith

I never questioned for a second that the project wouldn't work and I think that's one of the most important factors in its success to date. Having said that, we had no idea just how successful it would be, including the book. When Change the World for a Fiver was published we thought we'd maybe sell about 10,000 copies if we were lucky. It sold 100,000 copies in 100 days! When it was launched we had this fantastic breakfast with the Chancellor, and a big table full of business leaders. By the end of that breakfast we had sold 34,000 copies.

Another factor in the overall success has been having a wonderfully effective team. We have around us a group of people who share our belief and our passion and who work hard on the project. They share ownership of it. We have a formal team, who work with us on a day-to-day basis and then we also have an informal network of supporters who are there when we need them. So we're very blessed in that respect.

It's incredible how different my working environment is now from how it used to be in the corporate sector. A slight hangover from my corporate life was for a while, me thinking that everyone should automatically be in at 8 o'clock in the morning and work until 7 o'clock at night without talking or having fun. Whereas our team now range from full-time to part-time to 'if I feel like it' – which definitely isn't to say uncommitted! It's just that we each have very different styles of working, some more haphazard than others. But they're all so gorgeous and committed when they come in that I wouldn't have it any other way. It's so much better to allow people to be themselves at work. I mean, why should we change when we're in the working environment? Everyone has a good day, a grumpy day, a great day, a day when you want to work really hard and a day when you don't. I feel so incredibly proud when we're all there and everything's humming along.

Carpe Diem!

I don't think I'd do anything differently if I had the chance to do it all again although I can see that I went down quite a lot of dead ends at the beginning, spent a lot of time going into meetings and pursuing things which even at the time I instinctively never thought were going to get anywhere but was too polite to say. But having said that, I think that you should seize every opportunity you can because you never know what will come of it. So even if an encounter or a meeting doesn't bring the opportunity you wanted, you've made another contact and you just never know, something may come of it in the future.

In those early days when the phone rang, I was there. Any time. I never turned down an opportunity to meet someone or talk about the project, ever. And I worked pretty long hours. It very draining, because you're bringing people on board and trying to motivate and enthuse. This time last year I was going home, dropping my bags and reaching for the glass of wine as soon as I got in the front door!

Of course I'm still just as enthusiastic now as I was then – it's just that the priorities have changed. Now, we're pretty certain that this movement is going to go on and on and continue to be very

successful. So the challenge is now more about managing that enthusiasm and channelling it so we're not pulled in all directions. You need to have a certain amount of discipline. Some of the projects in the pipeline include working with the European Commission, doing some work with Coca-Cola, and maybe having another breakfast with the Chancellor. So with all these new possibilities, the job for the team is now to steer things in the right direction so we're not all over the shop. Knowing that we've gone from fragile to robust is a wonderful feeling. That's not to say we can't cock it all up, just that it's less likely now.

Don't just sit there!

I really believe that taking action when you're feeling down is the best thing. In fact, my hot tip is go and do something for somebody else. When my boyfriend was away on holiday recently, his neighbour who'd had a shitty week, went round and cleaned his house from top to bottom. I couldn't believe my eyes when I went in the door. But she did it because it she needed something to make her feel better - and it worked. And goodness knows it made me feel wonderful. So the moral is, if you're feeling shitty, come and clean my house. Or perhaps that should be, just do something for someone. I promise you you'll feel so much better for it.

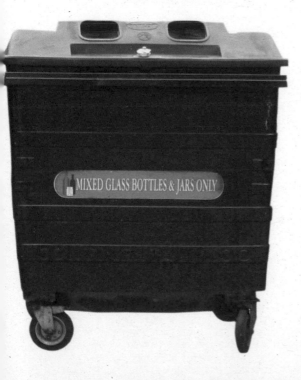

Ideas you can steal

Be positive!

Many social campaigns that aim to inspire people into action do so by telling you how terrible the world is. Worthy, negative, guilt provoking and generally serious tones define so much of the communication in the voluntary sector and the result is that people put 'doing good' firmly in a 'no fun zone'. Eugenie has ignored this tradition and blown away the cobwebs around activism, both in terms of what she wants us to do, and how she tells us to do it. This is more than a refreshing change; we think allowing people to smile while they change the world actually makes activism a more sustainable pursuit.

Something for everyone

Not everyone can be a full-time social entrepreneur, yet many campaigns take an all-or-nothing approach to enrolling support. This only serves to disincentivise anyone who can't go the whole hog, and it generates a kind of ethical elite who can afford to wear hemp and survive on organic leaves. Eugenie offers a range of activities so that everyone can do their bit, and everyone can have a positive experience of activism. Plus, who knows where somebody who's given a manageable introduction to activism will end up? First-time recycler today, tomorrow...

Don't be ashamed of not having 'suffered'

There can be an unhealthy trend around the voluntary sector of not welcoming people to contribute if they aren't perceived to have 'suffered'. Equally, people who'd like to help out often feel 'liberal guilt' if they haven't got a working class grandparent and didn't grew up on an estate. Both these issues only serve to exclude some very capable people from creating a positive impact, and Eugenie totally ignores them when she describes her own motivations. Social entrepreneurship is about passion and ability and not social qualifications, so don't let any lack of 'suffering' hold you back.

Trust that instinct will take you there

Although Eugenie wasn't clear for many years about the direction she wanted to go in, she never gave up on that gut feeling that somehow things should be different and that she had something to contribute. She persisted right through to the end, despite her career taking her in different directions at times. Drive and vision sometimes need to be accompanied by patience and faith that it'll work out in the end.

Norma Redfearn

West Walker Primary School: when Norma arrived in 1986 at the failing Tyneside school it was two thirds empty of pupils and located in one of the UK's most deprived areas. When she left in 2000 standards had improved by 300%, there was a waiting list for some year groups and the school had become a catalyst for regeneration in the local community.

Why she's here...

We think Norma is a rare breed and almost a contradiction in terms; a public sector entrepreneur. She possesses instincts we associate with commercial success which are unfortunately often lacking in public services: risk taking, innovation, and a responsiveness to need rather than convention; but she can also manoeuvre politically and engage a local community. This combination really sets Norma's work apart as 'social entrepreneurship plus'. A measure of her extraordinary success can now be seen in the government's Extended Schools policy which we think is attempting to recreate what Norma started back in 1986.

?WHAT IF! UnLtd*

Who is Norma Redfearn?

- Norma was born in Wallsend, Newcastle Upon Tyne, and her father worked in the local shipyards. She was the first person in her family to go to university, and went on to teach in inner city areas for 30 years.

- In 1997 she was awarded a prize for Public Leadership by the Office of Public Management, and in 1998 was chosen by the think-tank Demos to serve as an example of civic entrepreneurship.

- Norma is now an elected member of North Tyneside Borough Council and Cabinet Member for Children's Services and Families. She is also an Executive Member of the Tyne and Wear Play Association.

The issues she confronted

- The shipyards near West Walker were closed down in 1978 and industry was not regenerated; this sent the area into a spiral of economic and social decline.

- When Norma was appointed head teacher in 1986 70% of pupils qualified for free school meals, the school was half empty of students and was failing against national standards on attendance and achievement.

The solution she created

- Norma has turned the school and the local area around. She created a community wing offering: a café, social services provision, and an adult education centre, as well as a play park, a wildlife garden, a breakfast club and a community-designed and managed housing estate.

- There is now a waiting list to get into West Walker, attendance is up from 80% to 95%, and results have improved three fold.

Norma's story

The only way was up

West Walker is in an area of extreme social deprivation; to set that in context, we once had a lovely bright eight year old girl who couldn't come into school for two weeks because her teenage brother had sold all her shoes to buy drugs; this is how bad it is for some people in West Walker.

When I started out the school was on the verge of closing. We had a head count of 137 when our capacity was 300. Attendance was at 79% when the national target was 95%. Some children used to come in at about 10am, not because they wanted to learn but because they wanted their lunch. The school grounds were used to dump old settees and carpets, the classroom windows were always broken and classrooms were often set alight over night. The parents weren't supporting the school because many of them had failed in education. The local landscape was covered in derelict buildings left to die since the local shipyards closed. Our children were aged from just three years old and this was the environment in which they were supposed to learn.

I had one very simple aspiration: I wanted our children to achieve so that their talent would not be wasted. I wanted to make sure that when they left us to go to high school they had the basic skills to cope, to not feel inferior, and to at least have the chance to go on in education.

I also had a simple theory: we could only improve the education of the children by improving the whole community; it wouldn't work if I simply said I've got great teachers and we just teach children. If children are hungry and have no pencils at home, you can't teach them. If they live on a bloody awful housing estate where the people next door are on drugs and the atmosphere is full of depression, you can't teach them. When there's no interest in learning within their family, it's very hard to teach them. This was the reality in West Walker, so if we wanted the children to achieve, if we even wanted them to show up, we had to improve the whole community.

Making a connection

Our first step was really simple. There were a few parents who would hang around outside the gates when they dropped their children off, so I started to invite them in for a coffee and a chat. I would ask them what they wanted from the school and they were overwhelmed: 'Nobody has ever asked us what we think'. I told them it was their school, their children came here, and it belonged to them not me. Some of the staff whispered stuff like 'is she paid to drink coffee and chat with parents?' but I realised I could create a relationship and build trust with the parents by doing this.

After about three months I had half a dozen parents who would come and tell me what was worrying them. They'd say things like: 'I'd really love my child to do well, but I didn't do too well at school, I played the wag'; 'There's no jobs round here so what's the point?' or: 'I can't read Mrs Redfearn, so why are you sending these reading books home?'. Although we weren't solving any of these issues yet, we'd at least got them to open up.

The next step was to get these parents together with the rest of the school community so we held a planning day. The Chair of School Governors wasn't altogether convinced we'd get them to turn up, so my job that morning was to go from door to door collecting them all in my car and chauffeuring them in. This meeting really was where it all started. We had about 20 parents, along with the teachers, governors and the caretaker. We had some wonderful ideas, and more importantly we'd got everyone involved.

Not everyone pulling in the same direction

This idea of working alongside the parents was quite alien to some of the teachers, and at that first meeting there was a bit of 'what are they doing here?'. There was also an underlying attitude of 'not another initiative'. It was understandable considering the environment they'd been working in.

Much more disappointing was the reaction of the local authority when I invited them to the meeting. I rang the man in the local planning department and told him what we were all about: 'I need your help. We're going to look beyond the school to improve the surrounding areas and to try and make a difference for these people'. There was this long silence, and he said: 'Mrs Redfearn, you just look after the teaching and I'll tell you what you're going to have down there'. I put the phone down and said, 'bugger him!' Until that point I had been naïve enough to think that if I was excited by something that would make a difference, other people would automatically want to help us. How wrong I was.

Getting started

In the absence of the man from the planning department I had to look elsewhere for help at our meeting. I called a friend who was an architect, explained what we were doing, and that we barely had enough money for pencils. She was great, came along to our meeting and became a big part in everything we did.

The first thing the parents told us that day was that there were no play facilities in the area. This was true; a couple of my children

Staff Information

City of Newcastle upon Tyne
Walker School

Tony Broady, MA BSc DEA C Math FIMA FRSA
Headmaster

Walker School
Middle Street
Newcastle upon Tyne
NE6 1XY

Telephone: (0191) 262 0911
Fax: (0191) 263 6758

Congratulations to all staff

6 July 1998

Mrs N. Redfearn
Headteacher
West Walker Primary School
Church Street
Newcastle upon Tyne NE6 3XB

Dear Norma

Suffolk Reading Test Scores

Not only was your school the top performer by a long way in the Year 6 group 5b reading scores, it was also ahead of every single school in groups 4 and 5b and ahead of all except three in group 3 and all except the top six in group 2.

Whilst this says a lot about your pupils, it says far more about you and your staff. Your pupils are very fortunate that they attend your school and are taught by such outstandingly good teachers.

Yours sincerely

Tony Broady

had had terrible accidents playing in the derelict shipyards, largely because their families couldn't afford to pay for them to play somewhere safe. If we built a play area within the school grounds we could use it during the week, and parents could use it at weekends and in the holidays. My friend the architect wanted the children and the parents to help in the design, so a couple of her team came to the school over about six weeks and worked on the process of designing, building models, and writing letters to the relevant people. We incorporated all this in the children's different classes and it was a fantastic experience. We finished with a wonderful display and a lovely model that the children and the parents presented to the governing body. They did such a great job that the Chair of the Governors referred us to a committee at the Civic Centre called Inner City Partnerships to see if they'd fund the building of the playground. We were on our way.

So up we went to the ivory white tower, and the parents and the children got to go on the red carpet and sit in the red leather seats and were given tea in white bone china cups; my God this was fantastic. In they went and told their story and showed their model. When they were done the committee were so impressed that there was this group of people who wanted to change things where they lived, that they gave us £178k to build our play park. That group of parents and children who had walked in absolutely terrified, came out chests pumped up. Now that was grand.

The play park was all finished in 1989 and incredibly we won first prize for community development from the Royal Institute of British Architecture. A group of parents and children went down to London to meet Prince Charles, and when they came back we had a huge party and invited every child, parent and grandmother in the area. We had the full works; a bouncy castle, ice cream vans, lots of press and the local MP and councillors all came down. The man from the planning department even came along to say what a great job we'd done and how he'd always known it was a good idea. I was absolutely speechless, but him aside this was a huge occasion for West Walker. I think that was the point when the community realised that they could actually change things, and it was on the back of that success that we went on to do some great things.

Onwards and upwards

Our next project was to look at a corner of the school grounds used by the local glue sniffers. There was this little brick building and my first job every morning with the caretaker was to shift the glue bags before the three and four years olds arrived. We asked the children what they wanted in the space and they said they wanted a wildlife garden; so we built a wildlife garden. This time I didn't go to the man in the planning department, I just rang my architect friends and again they worked with the parents and children. The parents and children wrote off to loads of different charities and raised £5k, and before long we had a wildlife garden. I remember we got loads of criticism for putting in wooden picnic tables: 'Fancy using wooden tables, what a waste of money. If you build things out of wood they'll just be burnt down'. Those wooden tables are still there today.

Next, with more parents taking an interest in the school I decided to move things around a bit so as to free up one of the school

wings for community usage.

We organised a bunch of teachers, parents and children to go around the local streets knocking on doors and asking what the community wanted from the space. They said that there was no place to get a cuppa, so could we start up a café? This sounds a bit trivial but it was a great idea; parents who were dropping their children off in the morning could meet up over a coffee and share their issues; the elderly who are locked in horrible flats could come in for a break. It would be a really nice addition to the area. So, we managed to raise £16K to change one of the classrooms into a café, the local college trained a group of parents in food hygiene, and we opened a café.

The result was me being in trouble! 'A café, you've opened a café?' was the response of the local authority, 'You can't have a café in a school.' But of course they couldn't think of a good reason why we shouldn't open a café except that it had never been done before. In our opinion if it was good for the community it was good for the parents, and therefore it would be good for the children. So we did it.

As people started to use the café, they began chat to me. I kept hearing people say: 'Norma I wish I hadn't played truant, I wish I'd got stuck in at school', so I wrote to the Principal at a college in Newcastle to say I had a number of parents who wanted to get back into the learning game. I got no response so I went down there and knocked on his door. I told him about the parents and how I wanted his help. He wanted me to send them up to the college, so I said to him: 'Send them up? They've got no self-confidence, they're not going to come to a big college like this. I want you to send somebody down to our community wing'. 'Ah' he said, 'we don't do that'. I subtly explained that there were thousands of people out there who wanted to go back to learning, and the college should be prepared to help them do so. He phoned a few weeks later and said he'd sort something out, and soon we were providing adult education courses. Over the years it's grown from basic skills and assertiveness training, to first aid courses, classroom assistance qualifications, crèche workers' certificates, GCSEs and IT skills.

Through all the frustrations it's often been those adult courses that have given me the real highs. One day a woman who'd been in one of our basic skills classes came up to me, she was aged 47, and told me she'd just learnt to write her name for the very first time. And then she said to me: 'Norma I'm gonna come back tomorrow and I'm gonna get me a reading book'. One of the parents we took to meet Prince Charles in 1989 is now Assistant

Head in a local high school, and others have qualified as social workers, classroom assistants, crèche workers. It's great.

We also got a social worker placed in our community wing. We called her our Family Support Worker, and she was able to take on a lot of the problems that my staff and I were facing every morning. This freed us up, and gave the children the right support from a professional.

The next challenge was to look at attendance. By 1994 we'd improved from 79% to 88.4% which was good, but we needed to be nearer 95% to meet government targets. We knew that lots of the children were absent because they were getting sick, and especially in the mornings, so a good idea might be to set up a breakfast club. When I rang the Department of Health and explained our situation, their response was: 'Ah Mrs Redfearn we understand your problem, but nutrition really hasn't got anything to do with the Department of Health'. Well, if nutrition's got nothing to do with the Health Service, who the hell has it got something to do with?

But I'd decided that we were going to have a breakfast club anyway so I started knocking on the doors of local businesses and every term I would find £500 for the Breakfast Club. We had fruit juice, toast and jam, a choice of cereals, hot chocolate in the winter and yogurt in the summer, and we had parents and grandparents serving. The breakfasts were so good we once caught a boy who was supposed to be off with chickenpox coming in to get his breakfast, and then going back to bed without telling his mum! We started our Breakfast Club in 1994 with 20 children, and when I left 85 children were coming in for breakfast every morning. By 1999 our attendance was up to 95%.

Around that time I had a phone call from Business in the Community (BiTC) who had heard about what we were doing and wanted to bring a group of Chief Executives to West Walker to learn about community regeneration. 'Of course you can come, and bring them for breakfast' I said, 'they can have a slice of toast and a mug of tea like the children'. So they turned up and had a great time with our children. At the end of the day the MD of Greggs the bakers, Mike Darrington, told me how much he'd enjoyed his visit and he could see we were making a difference. I thanked him and said that as he was in charge at Greggs he could give us the bread for the Breakfast Club. A few weeks later he rang to say 'Norma you don't have to find the cash every term any more'. He's funded our Breakfast Club ever since, and when I retired he asked me if I would help me to set up Breakfast Clubs in other schools. There are now 100 Greggs Breakfast Clubs around the UK.

On another BiTC trip I cornered a guy and asked if he would give us his old office computers. He said yes and we set up a computer room for the children and the parents.

By now we had this nice school that wasn't being broken into or set fire to, and we had a play park and a lovely nature park. Our environment was beginning to be what a child deserves when they go to school, but opposite the school there was the broken-down remains of the old West Walker school. It had been there for 170 years but no-one had thought to knock it down so it was a real eyesore as you walked down the street. The parents said they wanted some nice new housing there, and as luck would have it the corporation who controlled the land was obligated to develop it with local community groups, so when we contacted them they grabbed us with both hands. The Tyne and Wear Development Corporation spent the next two and half years planning and building this new estate. The parents were fully involved in designing the houses, and they were taken to other estates to help them decide what they wanted. They settled upon quality, mixed housing, no dark passages, and they wanted big kitchens because that's where they spent most of their time. It was built and the local community manage it. Now when you walk down the street the view is wonderful.

At the same time the local council decided to get rid of the derelict shipyard and develop a riverside park. I offered the park warden an office in the community wing and within two weeks he wanted a classroom for a field study centre. Now he runs a weekend nature club, a photography club, and takes the children on bike rides.

A real impact on the community

When the Breakfast Club was up and running the local GP called wanting to know about all the people now working at the school and if there were any more jobs going. Apparently the lady who ran the Breakfast Club had come off her blood pressure tablets, another lady involved at the school had come off Valium for the first time in years, someone else had stopped complaining about her back. This was all because people had something to occupy them, and something to care about.

The positive relationship we'd created was clear: by 1999 we hadn't had any break-ins or any fires, and it had been great, and then a real test came. One morning I came in to find all our new computers had been stolen, £20K's worth gone. I wrote a letter home to all the parents that night saying how upsetting it was that people wanted to steal from their children, and the next morning I got a call saying to look in such and such a garage. Our community policeman checked it out and within a few hours he was borrowing five of our children to help carry the computers back to the school. To get those computers back within 24 hours really shows you the trust we'd built up. Plus, 18 months later when the guy who stole them had been released, he came to apologise and to ask if I would mind if his two children came to West Walker.

Spreading the word

With all our success we had interest from everywhere. The education establishment were coming to see us all the time, a

delegation came from Norway, a TV crew from Germany came to find out how we'd improved attendance, we appeared in the Japan Times, and I spoke at a conference in Atlanta Georgia about reducing deprivation.

Now the government is setting up what they call Extended Schools to address exactly what we were concerned with back in 1986: making schools a centre around which we can re-establish communities and provide local services. Local people came to our café for a cuppa, and so did the local bobby; the relationship that emerged meant that he suddenly knew everything that went on in the community. The school nurse would also pop in for a coffee, and soon people felt so comfortable with her that the local doctor reported a drop in her waiting list. I'm really hopeful that the government's plans will have the same successful impact on communities as we've enjoyed.

What I'm up to

After I retired I got involved with Tyne and Wear Play Association which puts play facilities like our play park into areas of deprivation. I also decided to go into politics so that I could continue to help the community, and a year ago was elected to the North Tyneside Borough Council. This year I became Cabinet Member for Children's and Family Services; I've been in that post for just a fortnight so I'm not sure what's going to happen, but I know something will happen! I also do talks which are supposed to be inspirational and motivational; 'Norma's coming in and she'll inspire you'; I think that's a load of rubbish but never mind.

My top tips

"Someone once said to me, 'success is not just about intelligence or creativity it's about determination and perseverance'."

"Be prepared for negativity and set backs, but carry on regardless."

"Keep your eye on a simple ultimate goal; for me that was getting my children to achieve, but get there by going step by step rather than with one fundamental shift. Everything we did was when a need was identified: the children were getting sick because they weren't eating well, so we gave them a breakfast club; parents had only negative experiences of school so we gave them a community wing and opened a café."

"Get the people you're trying to affect involved in the process. When we asked the parents and children for their input some ideas were great, some not so great, but what mattered was that they were participating in the process. That process built such a lot of trust between us."

My call to arms

"People in authority: reflect more on best practice and constantly reassess what you're doing. Too many times on my journey I came across people set in their ways and causing obstruction for no good reason."

"Service providers: focus more on the needs of the people you serve. Banks used to close at 3 o'clock, but every bugger was at work, and finally someone realised they should look at their hours. If you've got a service to deliver, find out what the needs are out there, and do whatever it takes."

"Give leaders enough licence and support them if they are prepared to take risks. Don't obstruct them on their journey. Be prepared to listen and if it's a worthwhile thing get on board and support them."

"Get away from paperwork and box ticking. Judge people by their results and the impact they create, not because they've ticked certain boxes."

Ideas you can steal

Be brave; ask or you don't get

Norma continually 'went direct'. She knocked on doors for cash, if someone didn't return a phone call she would turn up at their office, and when influential people were nearby she asked them outright to help. She is a great example of being brave and being direct.

Make your solutions real

Norma always made sure that when a presentation needed to be made to a funding body it was given by the parents and the children. By having 'the end user' present the project, the decision makers could see immediately that the community was on board. In effect the result of community regeneration had been achieved before a brick was laid.

Constantly question

On several occasions Norma was confronted by a brick wall answer: 'you can't do that', 'we don't do that', 'that's never been done before'. Her response was always to rebuff 'that' with 'why?', and she wouldn't give up until she was given a proper answer. To always ask 'why' is the route to creative thought, and that's why children are so creative because they won't accept convention as a reason for something to be. Always ask why, and then you get innovation.

Surround yourself with friends

Norma has incredible drive and determination, but she also had some wonderful friends. Her Chair of Governors was a constant support and when the 'man from the planning department' rejected West Walker she called in personal friends. Seek out great supporters and keep them close.

Carne Ross

Independent Diplomat: provides diplomatic representation for new nations, marginalised groups and others who struggle to make their voices heard on the international stage.

Why he's here...

In establishing Independent Diplomat, Carne put his neck on the line by giving up an illustrious career with the British Diplomatic Service. In the face of scepticism from all corners he persisted with his vision and in doing so, has rewritten the rules of diplomacy. Carne is providing expert diplomatic advice to those who need it most: the politically oppressed and economically marginalised. At the same time he is challenging the status quo of diplomacy being an elitist, secretive process, dominated by powerful governments.

Who is Carne?

Carne was born in London in 1966. After graduating from Exeter University he joined the Foreign Office's graduate fast-track programme. During his career in the Diplomatic Service he has held numerous positions including speech writer to the British Foreign Secretary, Middle East 'expert' (with the rank of First Secretary) for the UK delegation on the UN Security Council, and Strategy Coordinator for the UN in Kosovo.

He has drafted and negotiated several important Security Council resolutions, such as SCR 1284 which rewrote the Council's Iraq policy and established UNMOVIC, the weapons inspection body. He negotiated for the UK the resolution establishing the International Security Assistance Force (ISAF) in Afghanistan and the Council's resolution of 12 September 2001, condemning the attacks of the preceding day.

Carne resigned from the Diplomatic Service in 2004 to become an 'independent diplomat'. He is a trained negotiator and economist as well as a playwright and author. He is married and lives in London and New York.

The issues he confronted

Conventional diplomacy is a tool traditionally used by powerful governments to promote and protect their interests on the world stage; it is a process shrouded in secrecy that is normally out of reach from the 'underdog'.

Much of the world regards itself as marginalised on the international stage. Many governments and political groups, especially the poor and oppressed, are inexperienced in diplomatic techniques.

The solution he's created

Launched in 2004, Independent Diplomat is the first of its kind in the world: 'a diplomatic service for those who need it most'. It is independent of all government and international institutions, and is available to disadvantaged and marginalised clients.

Independent Diplomat is led by Carne and backed by a board of seven experienced and senior former diplomats, international lawyers and independent specialists; its consultants are drawn from a pool of high level ex-diplomats and political figures, as well as academics and policy analysts.

Carne's aim is for the organisation to grow into a global network of international advisers.

Carne's story

I was interested in the world 'out there' at quite a young age and decided early on that I was going to become a diplomat. Many people tried to discourage me, saying it was incredibly difficult and that you needed to be exceptionally clever. But after at least one attempt, I got into the Foreign Office's graduate fast-track programme.

I've worked in many different fields as a diplomat. I've been posted in Germany, Norway, New York and Afghanistan for varying periods and had many different roles, from speech writer for the Foreign Secretary to managing Britain's policy on the Arab/Israel dispute. I've been embroiled in wars, terrorism, arms control, a lot of the big issues that the world confronts today.

Reading between the lines

What became very clear to me was that the world of diplomacy is extremely difficult to penetrate and find your way around if you're an outsider of whatever kind, and particularly if you're a group of people who are not powerful, who are oppressed or marginalised in some way. That was really the inspiration behind Independent Diplomat: I knew that diplomacy was unnecessarily stuffy and obscure and that it needed an agency which would help these people navigate their way around.

The whole process of setting up Independent Diplomat was both gradual and a bolt out of the blue. It began with a gradual process of disillusionment with my own role as a civil servant of the British Government. I didn't really believe in the objectives of being a British diplomat; I didn't believe in the idea of State diplomacy, that somehow I as a British diplomat could articulate or represent Britain's interests. I find this whole way of thinking about diplomacy basically false.

I guess the real disillusionment set in during the mid-1990s with the civil war in Yugoslavia. Britain's reaction - to call it a civil war and react with an arms embargo - was unfair on the victims of aggression and was, in its effects, wrong and inhumane. It effectively gave the green light for one group to attack another with horrific consequences. The war was based on an invented Serb nationalism whipped up by Milosevic in his bid for power.

I faced a similar crisis of conscience in the run up to the war in Iraq. I regretted my role in the sanctions imposed by the British and American governments on Iraq: they harmed the Iraqi civilian population and had scant effect on the leadership they were supposed to pressure. We were aware of that damage at the time, but we didn't do enough to address it. I had my own part to play in that because I was a defender of British policy in the Security Council, and I'm not proud of that. We wouldn't have treated a European or American people in that way.

I was also pretty shocked at the way the government claimed that Iraq was a threat. I'd been reading the intelligence on Weapons of Mass Destruction for four and a half years, and there's no way that it could support the case that the government was presenting. We all knew that, we all believed the Iraqis had some kind of weapons and that they hadn't accounted for their past stocks, but there was in no way enough evidence to make a claim of imminent threat. The 45 minute stuff was ludicrous.

Giving up the day job

In the summer of 2004, I gave evidence for the Butler inquiry, which really was the nail in the coffin for my career in the civil service. That testimony summed up what I felt about the Iraq issue, and once I'd written it I knew there was no going back, I knew I couldn't work for this government and sleep well at night. I had to quit. Although that was unquestionably the right decision, it was still an extremely painful one. I had always wanted to be a diplomat and felt very sad that this is what it had come to.

I suppose the bolt came in March 2004 when my wife Karmen and I were in Istanbul. The idea came to us (well to my wife if I'm honest!) that we could set up a freelance diplomatic consultancy which would transform the way diplomacy is perceived and structured – it would be a completely different vision of diplomacy, one that wasn't led by governments but rather by groups of people. I think that in this respect, Independent Diplomat is unique. If you are a well-off government, you can find PR agencies or law firms who will help you represent yourself internationally, but the idea is a totally new one of a global network of diplomatic advice and expertise that will be available to the marginalised and the disadvantaged. And that was that; it was a kind of epiphany which in a big way crystallised a lot of what I'd been feeling about how diplomacy should be. The idea took hold and I began to develop it.

In general, it's quite hard to characterise who our potential clients are, but case by case it's much simpler to define. For example, the Kosovo government is facing a very complicated diplomatic process to determine the country's final status, so we're giving them expert advice on how to negotiate that process. We're also trying to help raise awareness of the Saharawi people, displaced by Morocco's long-standing occupation of the Western Sahara. Without a just resolution for the Saharawi people, the whole region could easily become destabilised again. That's one of the things that's so important about what we're doing: forcing those people in my world, in diplomacy, to recognise that there's an enormous need for this type of approach. We're being really inundated with requests for help from different groups around the world who would welcome advice on how to find their way through the diplomatic maze.

The hard slog

I've come across some enormous challenges from the beginning, the most obvious and basic one being lack of money. You can't live on fresh air. I gave up a secure job with a pension and a career structure and, I guess, status and worked for nothing for eight months to get things started. I didn't have any funding from anyone, not a bean, and that was hard. That was the biggest challenge. And, while a lot of people within diplomatic circles realised there was a need for the organisation, we came across quite a lot of scepticism about something new. Everyone agreed that yes, there is clearly a need, but why you? What can you do about it? And the advent of Independent Diplomat in different political settings has not been entirely welcomed by traditional actors; they don't take very kindly to the concept of somebody who doesn't have a conventional viewpoint being involved in such a traditionally structured process.

But I do believe that will gradually change because part of our objective is to change the way people think about diplomacy, to change the very terms of it. Merely by existing we're doing that.

I think that the need for Independent Diplomat is self-evident: the world is unfair and is tilted towards powerful people. Is the sky blue? There's a need for it. The only thing is, what's become very clear to me, is that the organisation needs to be a lot bigger to fulfil that need. I can't do it like I am now. I'm working very hard and I need more help, I need to build up a solid, international network.

I've recently won a 'Visionary' fellowship from the Joseph Rowntree Foundation which means that I'll be relatively financially stable for the next five years, but it's still not enough. What I need now is to get a big lump sum which will mean I can hire people on a secure basis, rather than having to say 'OK, I can hire you for six months but beyond that, I don't know'. It's hard to get good people to work for you on that basis. And I've been approached by several good people who want to work with me, who share my vision.

Redressing the balance

I strongly feel that the only reason I'm doing this is to try and rebalance things in the world a bit, to try and help the people who are powerless and left out. I don't want to help the rich and the powerful. I'm not interested in giving advice to companies who want to find out how to sign an oil contract with Nigeria or do business in Abu Dubai, I'm interested in helping the opposition parties in Burma and Zimbabwe, the Polisario in Western Sahara or the Malawi government when it's locked in negotiations with the EU, or small governments that find themselves on the UN Security Council for temporary membership – those are the kind of people I'm really interested in reaching, the others can help themselves.

No regrets, just sleepless nights

If I did it all again, I don't think I'd do anything differently. Although I do think I should have spent less time worrying. I spent a lot of time agonising, went through many sleepless nights. I'm a neurotic and maybe that's the type of personality that makes this kind of thing work, because I do worry and I'm obsessive. But, on reflection, I could have saved myself a lot of tossing and turning. As for the future, I want Independent Diplomat to be internationally recognised, with scores of staff, a bit like the International Crisis Group which has a budget of $10 million and something like 17 offices worldwide. I'd like the organisation to be up and ready whenever someone needs us, say when they are facing a tricky negotiation or have come up for temporary membership of the UN Security Council.

Ideas you can steal

The endgame is not the only game; just starting creates impact too

It might be years before Carne reaches his vision and Independent Diplomat is a significant player in world diplomatic circles, but just by starting the venture he has redefined what it is to be a diplomat. One of the most established and traditional worlds suddenly has a new aspect, and it's making people think. So, start sooner rather than later because as soon as you as you start, you'll start creating impact.

No one's ever heard of the job title 'ethical diplomat'

For some people doing your bit follows an obvious path; most professions can be channelled to doing some pro-bono work for the common good, for others that path is not so obvious, but we think finding it is very important. Carne created what is essentially a new profession with his social entrepreneurship, a make-over of a diplomat. We think that the best way to have an impact is not for accountants to be planting trees and architects teaching kids to read; all great things, but lacking the quality of impact achieved when, like Carne, you stick to what you do best.

Teach old dogs your new tricks (whether they like it or not!)

Social entrepreneurs have to work alongside those traditional deliverers of social impact, government and charities. That means wading through some of the most bureaucratic and structured environments known to man, and on occasion it can also mean meeting scepticism and aversion to change. Carne has successfully defeated (or perhaps just ignored) the issue of the old guard not welcoming new solutions, and it's something every good social entrepreneur must learn to do. Whether you're facing a funding application, a legislative issue, or procurement policy, you will be frustrated by the traditionalists, but remember you exist for a reason; the traditional methods haven't worked and you represent the way forward. Meet frustration with determination, and the establishment will (eventually) change.

Fergus Chambers

Fuel Zone: a branded, public sector school catering service which has used high street methods to significantly increase the uptake of school meals in Glasgow, whilst at the same time making the meals healthier.

Why he's here...

We chose Fergus because of the way he worked with his political colleagues in Glasgow City Council to create radical changes in a very poorly performing public service. Plus, his approach to school dinners is very different from and predates that of Jamie Oliver, proving for us that there isn't just 'one way to do it'. Fergus's method was to copy private sector methods boldly, be better than the private sector at their own game, then direct partnerships with his corporate suppliers to make them more responsible. He ignored the critics who said there should be a divide between the commercial and public sectors, and created one of the smartest, most comprehensive delivery mechanisms we've seen in local government. Fuel Zone provides a model for change respected the world over, and its impact will be felt for years to come.

Who is Fergus Chambers?

Fergus was born in Glasgow in 1956, he graduated in 1977 from Glasgow College of Food Technology and embarked on a career in catering. He joined the CCG catering group where he undertook 18 different jobs in five and a half years, was headhunted in 1982 by Sutcliffe Catering (part of the P&O Group), and then joined Douwe Egberts coffee company.

Fergus joined Strathclyde Regional Council in 1988 where he co-developed Catering Direct, the first branded public sector catering organisation, and the largest in Europe with about 6,700 staff.

He is now Director of both Catering and Cleaning and Home Care Services for Glasgow City Council. These functions have a combined employee team of 9,100 people.

The issues he confronted

40% of the most deprived areas of Scotland are found in Glasgow City, and seven of the 10 UK political constituencies with the highest rates of premature deaths are located in Glasgow.

The average male in Glasgow will live 10.7 years fewer than the average male in the London Borough of Kensington and Chelsea.

When Fuel Zone started 36.2% of secondary school kids were entitled to free school meals, but only 63% of those meals were being taken up.

The solution he created

Fuel Zone has doubled the number of meals taken up, and on average a Fuel Zone school serves a child every four seconds during the 40 minute lunch break.

Fuel Zone has made eating in school cool. It has incentivised healthy eating, and it has been the spearhead for a range of healthy living initiatives across Glasgow and the rest of the UK.

Fergus's story

Our big picture

We created Fuel Zone by doing something different; we used lessons from the high street to radically modernise a failing, underinvested Glasgow public service. The overall impact is a healthier, happier city, and if we do something similar nationwide we'll end up with kids that enjoy school more and get better grades; we'll have kids that can enjoy physical activity and will live longer; and we'll have kids taking the healthy food message into the wider community network, all because we were brave enough to take a different approach; that's not bad!

No student protester

When we talk about the ethical or social impact of Fuel Zone I have to be honest and say that we weren't really looking for that at the start, and I was certainly never the student protester type. I joined the public sector in 1988 when the government introduced compulsory competitive tendering and needed to recruit people like me with private sector experience to help compete against the commercial operators. I arrived with a typical arrogance; 'the private sector knows best', but it didn't take me long to be humbled by the skills of the people I found in the public sector, and to be excited by the unique set of challenges you face there.

A failing business...

The Fuel Zone story started at the end of 1996 when local government was reorganised and suddenly my team was responsible for catering and cleaning throughout Glasgow. Our first task was to review the performance of each of our service areas and we found that school meals, as a business, was not trading well. There was poor demand, low self- esteem, lack of investment and things hadn't been modernised for many, many a year. Things were so bad that a large proportion of the children who qualified for free school meals didn't even actually take them up. So, from a purely business perspective we needed to revamp Glasgow's school meals service.

The first step was to talk to our customers, the kids. They told us in no uncertain terms what they saw as the three problems with school meals: queuing, the food, and the environment. Pupils hated how long it took to get served and having teachers patrol them while they waited; they didn't value the type of food that they were being served and felt it wasn't presented well; and lunch was served in an environment that wasn't modern or trendy or enticing to them in any way. I think that's when it struck us; we were serving up dinners to the toughest, most savvy consumers there are, teenagers, and we were 30 years behind current marketing thinking. In short, school dinners weren't cool.

...to the best there is...

So we did what they told us. My team and I went to the high street, saw what it was the kids were going for and then we quite simply stole every trick the commercial world had to offer. We didn't just have one till at the end of the shelf we put several tills behind the counter, we lit up bright menus above the hatch, we had the staff in new modern uniforms, and we served much more hand-held food. We knew that the high street stuff would draw some criticism but to my mind it was worth it. If we wanted to deal with health issues, we could only do it when we had kids actually turning up to the dinner hall. In the end taking that risk paid off; we ran a pilot in four schools for four months,

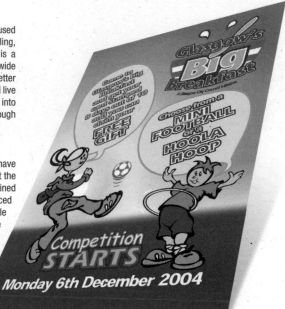

and at the end of that time each school was serving a child every four seconds. That is way beyond anything the high street attains, and we had more than doubled volumes in those schools. Any child going into one of those Fuel Zones saw a radical difference; it was no longer a traditional institutionalised, slow, un-trendy set-up, it was a modern sophisticated service and very fast.

...paid for by someone else

Having achieved this level of success in the pilot put us in great shape. We'd spent all of our cash converting those first four schools to Fuel Zones, but there were still 25 more to go. So we took a few deep breaths and bit the bullet; we sat down with our suppliers and politely pointed out that if they wanted to continue enjoying double volumes, they might like to invest in that success. To their great credit they responded, and gave us the capital to roll out the programme to the extra schools. In just over a year we'd opened 29 branded food service restaurants, paid for by the private sector.

Capping all that success is the Fuel Zone website (www.fuelzone.co.uk), something that I'm particularly proud of and which I think shows how confident and ambitious we've grown to be. It works in conjunction with a cashless system we'd introduced; all the children pay with a kind of debit card, meaning that no-one could tell who's on free school meals. The card also serves to record what a kid orders, and they earn points depending on how healthy their choice is; more points for the healthy option, and if they order the 'Vital Mix' which is the combination of the most healthy items, they earn maximum points. Each child has their own personal account held on the website where they can check their account, select their rewards (up to an iPod!), and have it delivered to their home. We have to incentivise the kids to make healthy choices because unhealthy food is still their habit. The effect it's had on our sales mix has been unbelievable.

A good dance with the devil!

That's basically the Fuel Zone chain of events, but I think the most innovative, entrepreneurial element is in how we went from first 'stealing' high street techniques to then actually driving partnerships with our private sector suppliers. We didn't stop at getting them to pay for our roll-out of Fuel Zone, we went on to fundamentally shift the way our suppliers worked with us, and how responsible they were when it came to working in schools.

The first step in this positive shift was to take every commercial brand identity out of Fuel Zones, including the likes of Coca-Cola, McCain, Birds Eye, Iron Bru… We sat down our suppliers and said: 'If we leave your brands in those schools there will be pressure to stop selling your products. We'd rather continue selling your products in a sensible manner.' Credit to them, they accepted this and allowed us to de-brand, which is quite something when you consider we're talking about some of the world's most recognisable companies. We replaced every Coke or Iron Bru cup with a Fuel Zone cup; where there were famous logos we now had Fuel Zone logos. Those brands co-operated because we'd doubled their sales, and because they recognised that the growing health agenda meant that branding in schools was a very sensitive issue.

Next came a whole new range of healthier menu items. We told them 'We still want to do business with you, but we want to influence what you supply us. We won't ban any of your products; we'll just incentivise healthier options and see what happens to the sales mix.' If they supplied us with high sugar carbonates we would promote their low sugar fruit drinks and waters, so our volumes with those same suppliers didn't go down but what we bought from them started to fundamentally change. We now buy half the amount of chips we used to which you'd guess would be bad news for McCain, but the children are buying loads of McCain pizzas. Pizzas might not sound particularly healthy but together with McCain we created and sourced a pizza with low fat cheese; that pizza is now a highly successful line throughout the UK. This is where we really added value; we stepped up to help suppliers develop the new healthier options. We became far better at forecasting the market and noticing trends because our team would constantly be on the high street finding out was going on with kids, and I travelled the world learning from best and worst practise elsewhere. We worked with one of the biggest UK hot dog manufacturers to produce a hot dog which met new nutritional standards in primary schools; that product is now being sold throughout the UK food service circuit. So, a humble council catering team was helping lead new product development for major commercial companies.

A big reason for the success of this relationship is that our suppliers showed a great deal of trust in us, and I really want to commend them for that. Again we found some people were opposed to us having close links with private companies, many of whom are associated with the health issues we face in Glasgow. But we've had a positive impact on those companies, and because of their scale we've actually been able to do more for kids' health than if we'd shut them out.

Telling the world

When we finally got a moment we opened our doors and invited local authorities from throughout the UK to have a look. 256 people came in one day. What's great is that many local authorities came and saw what we'd done and have now developed their own versions of Fuel Zone, showing for once that the public sector can share good practice and good ideas. The media response was absolutely unbelievable. We had TV crews visit from America (ABC), Japan (Fuji News which has 18 million viewers every night!), New Zealand, France, Sweden, Finland, umpteen film companies, and the BBC and ITN. We did probably a dozen live radio interviews, it went global with BBC World News and countless foreign articles all over the internet. It was a huge story.

Our impact

As Fuel Zone became more established we've been able to extend our reach and really impact on the health of Glasgow: we have someone from the NHS working with us to develop new initiatives around food, health and hygiene; we've launched the biggest free fruit programme in Western Europe, and the most extensive free breakfast service in Britain, which ensures every primary school child has the opportunity to come for a free healthy breakfast every morning; and we've invested £2million introducing plumbed, chilled, fresh water systems in schools so the kids are no longer dehydrated when they're trying to learn.

Since we launched the free fruit programme sales of fresh fruit and vegetables in local communities are booming because children are pestering their parents to buy apples and carrots instead of nuggets and chips; teachers and parents report that behaviour and attentiveness is better when the kids are hydrated and have something in their stomachs. Some other knock-on effects include happier catering staff because they enjoy feeding more children and they're wasting less food, and happier head teachers because more kids are staying to eat at school rather than going outside and causing problems in the community. It'll obviously take years if not decades to record our longer term impact on health issues in Glasgow such as low life expectancy and coronary heart disease but we're working closely with NHS Greater Glasgow to look at how we are affecting these problems.

We also create impact by sharing our knowledge and experience to help others to similarly improve school meals. Following our success with Fuel Zone I was made part of the team which undertook a study called Hungry for Success for the Scottish Executive looking at how to improve school meals in Scotland. That ended up with a £63million investment to pay for more food on the plate, healthier food, and a better nutritional balance. The government in England has now followed Scotland with some

money to improve school meals (in my opinion not enough) and as we speak is in the middle of trying to decide how it should be spent. Hopefully they'll look to learn from what we've achieved in Scotland.

A team effort

It's important to note that Fuel Zone was not the brainchild of one individual; I may have led the changes but it's been driven by a committed and highly skilled team at Glasgow City Council. Credit

also goes well beyond our single council catering team to the wider political establishment in Scotland who, with an eye on the disturbing obesity trends in America, boldly decided to make the health of its residents a long-term strategic priority. Our team may have started a great trend but that support from government has been essential, and considering Fuel Zone has been a fairly radical and some would say dangerous path to take, I think that support is pretty remarkable.

My top tips

"Never underestimate the power of good market research; without talking to children we never would have known that queuing was their number one issue with school meals, and that fundamentally guided what Fuel Zone became."

"Get your stakeholders to come and see what you're doing; have them experience, taste and touch whatever it is that you do. We did this with parents and they became our biggest advocates."

"Assemble around you a great team of people with the right range of skills and qualifications. Our team bring together a variety of skills and experience, and they hail from both the public and the private sector."

"Network to create change! If I know that the vice president of Coca-Cola is coming over to visit the East Kilbride plant, I'll invite him to play golf!"

My call to arms

"Suppliers of school meals need to get better and faster at new product development. We found that they weren't geared up to spot trends and they were slow to respond."

"Local authority catering teams need to spend more time 'outside the kitchen'. They need to have a look at other operations, nationally and internationally, and at research on health, obesity and food issues. We need to learn from the experiences of others, especially in America."

"We need to educate children at a young age about food. Home Economics is treated as a bit of a joke, the name doesn't make sense to kids and isn't exactly trendy; teaching is fragmented, and only done well in a small handful of schools. Yes let's continue to invest in school meals, but let's see similar levels of investment in actually trying to educate the parents of tomorrow in cooking food at home. School meals only represent between 8-14% of a child's diet over a year; it's only one meal out of three, five days out of seven, 39 weeks out of 52, and not all kids actually take school meals. Parents are responsible for the other 84%-92%. We must get parents away from convenience foods, and back to a situation where they have the skills to cook simple, cheap, healthy foods."

Ideas you can steal

You can't please all the people all the time

People want complete, flawless solutions to social issues, and when you appear to be doing something good or ethical their cynic switch will often flip. It's very difficult to deliver solutions which tick every single social and environmental box, and therefore you're bound to rub someone up the wrong way; maybe it's overly commercial, perhaps you're not using the latest eco packaging… We think you can only do so much, and perhaps attempting to do everything means you could end up doing nothing at all.

Cross sector partnerships are where it's at

We don't think that one sector, whether it be private, public or voluntary has all the answers; it's when you combine the best of different worlds that great solutions emerge. Fergus and his team established partnerships with the private sector, and adopted methods never previously used by a city council, and the result was more innovative and more impactful than it would have been had they kept to a traditional public sector approach. Ignore traditional roles and barriers; it's all about impact.

One thing at a time

Fuel Zone was criticised for not broaching the health issue from the start, but if they had they might have been preaching to empty dinner halls. They bit the bullet and used the pulling power of brands to bring kids back to school dinners, and then got onto promoting health. This is a case where the ends have certainly justified the means.

Amanda & Stephen Argent

Cats Clubs: a new concept in after-school clubs that combines childcare provision with educational support in an enjoyable environment. Starting in one school, it has been rolled out successfully to become a nationwide network benefiting both parents and kids.

Why they're here...

When Amanda and Stephen found themselves facing two of the most common issues confronting families today - the education of their kids and affordable childcare – they responded by developing what we think is an effective solution that cracks them both. Cats Clubs is a whole new breed of after-school club which combines an online educational computer programme to help improve kids' literacy and numeracy, with a fun place for kids to be. For us, Amanda and Stephen represent the reality for many social entrepreneurs who juggle family life with a burgeoning new enterprise. Having survived raising four young kids, late nights and tricky headmasters, Amanda and Stephen have developed a solution which provides a desperately needed service for kids and parents alike, in some of the most deprived wards in England.

Who are Amanda and Stephen?

- Amanda started her career working for Psion Computers before leaving in 1987 to have the first of her four daughters.

- Stephen is a chartered accountant and worked for a London accountancy firm before setting up his own practice. He has also started his own computer service company called Computer Troubleshooters and has been a contributor on computer issues for the Mail on Sunday.

- Amanda and Stephen set up Cats Clubs from their living room. By working from home they were able to spend time with their four daughters, while making sure their rapidly growing organisation was well taken care of. Amanda is Chief Executive of Cats Club and Stephen is the Chief Financial Officer.

The issues they confronted

- Research shows that children in some of the more deprived wards of the UK don't do as well at school as their better off counterparts; they are less likely to have computers at home so it's harder for them to catch up, and don't have the luxury of access to private tutors. Often the schools themselves are struggling to get children's literacy and numeracy rates up to the national standard.

- Only a very small percentage of children at school have access to after-school clubs; there aren't many around and those that are, rarely include integrated learning.

- The many parents who can't afford after-school childcare are often the ones who have to work longer hours or do shift work, so they really need a reliable, low-cost solution.

The solutions they created

- Schoolfriend is the first web-based, interactive, bespoke learning course for children aged between 4 and 13. It's enjoyable to use, the kids can progress at their own rate, and from just 99p per child per week it's also inexpensive. What's more, it works: an independent study by the Institute of Education showed that children's numeracy and literacy significantly improves when using Schoolfriend on a regular basis.

- By combining Schoolfriend with other learning based activities, Cats Clubs are keeping children engaged in the hours after school. It is now the largest charitable childcare organisation in the country.

The Cats Club story

My background is in computers; Stephen's a chartered accountant but his job also involves a lot of IT work. In 1987, I got pregnant with our first child and our brood started growing from there - we now have four kids. And that's where it all started I guess, where the whole inspiration for Schoolfriend came from - our experiences with our own kids. We started to see that what children at primary school level really need is the chance to go over things again and learn without pressure. We thought that we could use our own areas of expertise to make a real difference to children who needed that bit of extra help at school. It's fine if you can pay for a tutor to come to your house at £40 an hour, but the vast majority of people can't do that, it's just not feasible. So Schoolfriend was set up to be a private tutor on the computer, to be accessible to as many kids as possible.

Work hard, play hard

Schoolfriend's a web-based learning programme which is tailored to each child's needs. The idea is that children can earn downloadable, fun games as a reward for work done well. The whole aim is to encourage and entertain children in an interesting and stimulating way. We started developing Schoolfriend, with education specialists in 1999 and launched it in schools in 2000. That was really exciting, to see something that you've created yourself actually working. It was also pretty nerve-wracking as we didn't really know how it would actually work in practice.

The Cats Club stuff we literally fell into as we went around the country with Schoolfriend. The schools we went to had all these great facilities, nice big spaces that we could see weren't being used. I just happened to be chatting to a head at one of the schools, asked him what he did with the facilities at the end of the day, and he said "Nothing, we close up when the kids go home." And I thought, what a waste! So I asked him if we could use their IT facilities at the end of the day and he agreed.

That was a real start, but it soon became clear, mainly through word of mouth that the parents wanted more than that; they wanted proper childcare to last until six o'clock so they could do their work and then come and collect their kids at the end of the

day. So we decided to test this theory, and with funding from the New Opportunities Fund, sent out questionnaires to hundreds of parents to see exactly what they wanted for their kids. The response rate was overwhelming and the figures proved what we thought: around 95% of parents said they were worried about their kids' numeracy and literacy levels and also wanted the children to be looked after until 6pm, in a safe environment.

Schoolfriend in fact only runs for 20 minutes – if we just gave the kids that to do for three hours they'd be bored senseless, so that's when the childcare aspect came in to play. Basically, we wanted to make learning fun and for them to see that it doesn't have to always involve structured lessons and be boring. So I think we wanted to really put study into a new context, one that the kids could relate to.

We first set up a pilot club in one school in April 2003 in Northamptonshire which was really successful; that club's still running and is still going strong. In the end we piloted three schools before we got some funding, which we used to open another six Cats Clubs later that year in Northamptonshire. So we knew we had a model that worked. There was a lot of demand for Cats Clubs and there seemed to be funding available. But it was only the clubs that we got funding for so we were still working as volunteers. Plus we hadn't fully appreciated the operational obstacles of growing so quickly.

Start-up funding is generally available through local education authorities, but we have to make a club sustainable within its first year of operation. Of course, there are many times that we would like to reduce the childcare costs to parents, particularly in some of the more deprived areas. There are also extra activities that we would love to bring into the clubs but can't always afford to. So, we're always on the look out for sponsorship or additional funding that will allow us to go that extra mile.

Being a social enterprise means a lot of things to us. The 'social' thread runs through all that we do, through our practices and our ethos. Not only do we aim to make our services accessible to less well-off families, we also try to employ local people and improve communities that way.

That's really what got us interested in the social enterprise side of things; by employing people from local communities you're reducing unemployment in those areas and allowing people to go back to work or do longer hours if they need to, because they've got the childcare sorted. You also make a difference to the children because you're giving them a boost academically. Plus, the activities we do allows them to experience things they otherwise wouldn't have a chance to do, like a lot of creative stuff, arts and music and drama.

The true test

When we opened the sixth club we came across a whole range of issues that we hadn't appreciated fully after opening the first one. It is one thing to get the money to open new clubs, but then you actually have to make them work as well. Once you reach a certain scale, you can no longer just go with the flow; you have to build an organisation that can deal with that growth.

So the true pilot came about in September 2003, with the seventh club. Staffing was the main issue. That hasn't

changed; staffing is still a problem. It's a fairly new concept, 'play work', so it's difficult for us to get staff who have the qualifications we need. That's one of the things we're trying to address. We're going to have to develop our own staff, to take on unqualified people and train them up. That's the plan: we will grow our own workforce. But it doesn't happen over night, that's a long-term goal.

Another problem is that it's difficult for teachers to get out of teaching mode - so if we have teachers who work for us we have to explain to them that they don't have to take the register, etc. It's about changing the 'school' mentality which is very regimented, and making things more informal and less structured.

Going head first

Many of the other challenges we face are the same now as when we started: working with the schools, and having a good relationship with the heads. Some heads see the schools as their personal domains and although they very much want to be able to offer the service to their children, the idea that they are letting a third party into their school and that they don't have any say in how it's run is very difficult for some of them to get over. Also, the clubs are regulated under the Children Act, whereas schools run under the Education Act and the two systems are very different.

The whole point of the kids coming to the club is that they can chill out and do what they like within reason; it's a relaxed time for them and if they want to change out of their uniform they can. Some heads find that difficult, but the vast majority are extremely supportive. The reason that we want to base the clubs on school premises is that parents know it's somewhere familiar, and the kids too. I also really think that we should make the most of the schools; a load of money has been poured into our schools and then they just sit empty after 3.30pm which is absolutely ridiculous. It's such a waste of some excellent facilities; we felt passionately that they should be used. The challenge is trying to win those heads over.

Onwards and upwards

We've been overwhelmed by the demand for it all. The areas that we do best in are where the parents are working but they're not earning huge sums of money and certainly can't afford nannies. What they want is somewhere they know is familiar and safe and the kids are well looked after, and by giving them that your reputation spreads by word of mouth. I think that given a choice of having a childminder or a daily after-school club running on the premises until six o'clock, parents are going to choose the school club each time.

In the future we'd really like to expand into secondary schools, obviously using a very different set of activities and challenges. We'd also like to become the government's preferred supplier of childcare. We're setting a standard; we're the only people in the country who are rolling up our sleeves and delivering childcare on a national basis. Previously it's always been run by voluntary organisations, parents' committees, maybe a local group. But we're the first to roll it out nationally. UnLtd helped us produce a template using the concept of 'Cats Club in a Box' which has given us a formula to stick to as we go around opening further clubs. That's made things a lot easier for us; although we obviously have to tailor each club to the local community's needs.

On reflection

Hindsight's a wonderful thing isn't it? I think if we had it, we'd think 'look there's all this demand, but what we need to do is set up a core structure first' and then start to roll the clubs out. But because we didn't know what the demand was going to be, we opened each club one at a time, one after the other, and by September 2004 we had about 25 clubs. Our very limited infrastructure was having to cope with all of that. With hindsight I'd have built up the infrastructure first. But nobody could see it then. We were fortunate to get funding from Futurebuilders too, which has made a very big difference to us. Now, a strong infrastructure is helping us develop and support a very aggressive roll-out of clubs in line with the government's Extended Schools agenda.

The bottom line

I think - and this is a little ironic - that in order for a social enterprise to work you do have to be very commercial about it. At the end of the day the books have to balance; you just can't run at a loss. It's difficult; you're put in a difficult position because on the one hand it's a social enterprise which means you try to be sympathetic to everybody but on the other you do need a bit more of a hard-nosed approach. So for example, parents can't always afford to pay. So the social side of that is that you look at ways to help, you might look at weekly payment schedules and you can let it go for a couple of weeks until things are easier for them financially – but the commercial side of it, the reality, is that to make the clubs sustainable parents have to pay. So after so many sessions where they haven't paid we have to crack down and say "We're really sorry but we can't take your child". This is something that schools would find particularly hard; if they wanted to run a club themselves and parents aren't used to paying for their kids to go to school, it's not easy to then turn around and ask for money. But that funding is crucial. For the schools to have that hard-nosed commercial approach is extremely difficult. For us as an outside organisation it's easier. The bottom line is you do have to be commercially aware.

Burning the candle

We work incredibly long hours and go to bed extremely late at night. It's not uncommon for me to be checking my emails at 2.30 or 3.00am, and sometimes that takes its toll. In my case, because I took time out when the kids were very young – now the youngest is 10 and the oldest is 17 – it's easier to fit in the long hours. But it is a juggle, it is difficult and it is a compromise. The reality is that the reason I'm checking my emails at 3am is probably because I've taken a few hours out during the evening to be with the kids. So it's swings and roundabouts. It may not be easy but it is very rewarding, particularly when you receive letters from parents – as we do regularly – telling us what a big difference our service has made to their lives.

Tough love for sustainability

It can get a bit tricky when in a social enterprise you need to charge for an essential service, but a good social entrepreneur can see beyond that immediate discomfort so as to ensure the long-term success of a project. Amanda's honesty and single-minded attitude towards charging parents really struck us, and is an example to anyone who might feel a bit uneasy in a similar situation.

Replication is nirvana

It's the biggest challenge faced by those of us who support social entrepreneurs; how to make sure great projects scale up to create as wide an impact as possible. With Cats Club in a Box Amanda and Steve have met that challenge. They've isolated the principles of Cats Club and what it takes to reproduce the programme anywhere in the UK. Now it can and will grow with demand, and won't be constrained as many other projects are, by the personal reach of the entrepreneur.

Be on the look out for links

There's something wonderfully logical about how Amanda and Steve developed Cats Club: Schoolfriend only lasted 20 minutes and parents told them they needed after-school care, so they launched Cats Club; they needed a venue, came across a school that was empty after 4pm, so they held Cats Clubs in schools… Great entrepreneurs, whether they be social or commercial, always have their eyes open for links or other initiatives on which to piggy back. It was by doing this that Amanda and Steve turned a computer tutor into an extensive after-school initiative.

Gib Bulloch

Accenture Development Partnerships (ADP):
ADP has found a way to deliver world-class business consultancy skills to international development organisations at a price that the sector can afford. It allows Accenture staff to work for charities and non-governmental organisations (NGOs) whilst remaining within the company and continuing their careers.

Why he's here...

What Gib and his team have created is like a corporate volunteering scheme that has evolved out of sight of anything we've come across in current mainstream corporate social responsibility (CSR). We like ADP because it goes way beyond a token bit of tree planting or even allowing people to take sabbaticals; the model Gib and the team have created allows one of the most commercially minded companies on the planet to send their people to work professionally in the development sector. We think ADP's sustainable model is testament that there is always another way, no matter what economics appear to say or where traditional voluntary and private sector boundaries lie. He has proven that social responsibility makes business sense, especially when it comes to keeping the most talented people happy within an organisation.

Who is Gib Bulloch?

Gib was born and brought up on the Isle of Bute, off the west coast of Scotland. Both his parents were teachers and he studied Engineering and Naval Architecture at Strathclyde University (but has never designed a ship in his life).

After graduating in 1989 he joined BP Exploration in Aberdeen. He left to study for an MBA and then joined Mars in their sales and marketing team.

He joined Accenture in 1996 as a strategy consultant to telecoms companies, before moving into the oil and gas industry department.

The issues he confronted

The international development community needs to modernise and develop new approaches to the world's social and economic development challenges.

There is a limited view of what business can offer to the development sector; to date it has been a case of 'the best they can do is less bad'. Therefore business has often been sidelined from supporting development issues.

Private sector consultancy organisations like Accenture with very relevant expertise (supply chain management, IT systems, leadership development…) are far out of the reach of the development sector financially, and prior to ADP, there was no easy mechanism to bring the two 'sides' together.

The solution he's created

Accenture staff can apply to work on an ADP project after they have had three years' experience within the company. They live and work for 3 to 6 months in the development sector, normally in the developing world, and then go back to their normal role. ADP started in Accenture UK, but has since rolled out to 14 countries including France, the USA, South Africa and Australia.

ADP operates using a unique financial model with three-way contributions: Accenture provides people on a non-profit basis (plus access to premises, knowledge capital etc), the employee contributes in terms of a 50% reduction in salary, and the client NGO or a donor organisation pays a fee but at a fraction of market rates. This works out with ADP being non-profit making, but cost neutral to the main Accenture business.

At any one point there are 15 to 20 ADP projects underway, involving approximately 50 people stationed all over the world. Over 100 people will go through the programme each year. To date, ADP has completed over 60 projects in 34 countries across four continents involving over 130 people, and it's doubling in size each year.

Gib's story

A little itch

In the late 1990s there was a lot going on for me. I was having a great time working for Accenture in the oil and gas sector, I was earning well and in lots of ways I loved my job. At the same time issues were arising in the industry like Shell's operations in Nigeria, the environmental challenges around the disposal of the Brent Spar oil platform, the emergence of renewable energy… and I started to take an interest. Pay rises and promotions were meaning less and less to me and I developed what can only be described as an 'itch' that I couldn't quite scratch.

It was against this background that the epiphany came. I was travelling on the District Line at the time, so not exactly the road to Damascus. I was reading the FT (Financial Times) and there was this article about the role of business skills in development and how Voluntary Service Overseas (VSO) needed business people for a new short-term programme called Business Partnerships. I arranged a meeting with Michael Shann, the Programme Manager from VSO to find out more. We both laugh when we recall that first meeting – he dressed up in a suit and tie to meet me, I'd put on my jeans and a tee-shirt! At the time Business Partnerships was quite innovative and six years on still is: 'Big companies, we don't want your money we want access to your people'. It sounded perfect; if I could get Accenture to sign up to the programme I could go on a trip, scratch 'the itch', and return to everything I had at Accenture after six really fulfilling months.

Booking my ticket

So, how to get Accenture engaged? There was a guy in charge of the UK consulting business at the time called Willie Jameson, quite a fearsome guy by reputation. I got a 15 minute telephone slot in his agenda. He listened, asked some tough questions, thought for a moment, and then said: 'Right we'll do it. I'll get Human Resources involved, I'll get Finance involved, we'll set up the policy, and we'll do it', and that was literally all it took to sanction Accenture getting involved with VSO.

About a year after my conversation with Willie I was on my way to Macedonia to work in a small enterprise development facility near the Kosovan border. Overnight I went from the cut and thrust

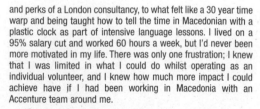

and perks of a London consultancy, to what felt like a 30 year time warp and being taught how to tell the time in Macedonian with a plastic clock as part of intensive language lessons. I lived on a 95% salary cut and worked 60 hours a week, but I'd never been more motivated in my life. There was only one frustration; I knew that I was limited in what I could do whilst operating as an individual volunteer, and I knew how much more impact I could achieve have if I had been working in Macedonia with an Accenture team around me.

The sum is mightier than the parts

There's a simple reason why I was in Macedonia as an individual rather than as Accenture; we and everyone in our sector are too expensive for the world of development. As my trip neared its end my mind was racing as to how I could stay involved; stay with VSO, move into international development… But if I stayed at Accenture, and got that Goliath of an organisation to move just one degree towards the development world the impact would be far greater than anything achieved by jumping the fence into the non-profit sector.

This for me is an exciting point. What were very exclusive worlds: for-profit, non-profit, public sector, government… are now beginning to blur at the boundaries, and where they overlap really impactful partnerships are starting to emerge. Business is beginning to play a role in social issues beyond its philanthropic cheque book, and leveraging other assets like scale, brand, people… This takes corporate citizenship forward from just being about compliance, to an exciting and unlimited future.

Going way beyond conventional CSR

But I digress; even towards the end of my time in Macedonia I was a novice in international development and cross sector partnerships were not the first thing on my mind. What was on my mind, along with a group of equally passionate colleagues including Jill Huntley who was also on VSO and was driving this as passionately as I was, was how we could make it possible for Accenture to go beyond allowing a handful of us to go on sabbaticals under a conventional, limited CSR banner. That basically meant asking how to get round the economic reality that the development sector just couldn't afford us. We needed to turn the existing Accenture business model on its head and strip out as many costs as we could. What we came up with was a concept that could channel business and technology skills to the developing world and provide what we called 'an integrated career option' to employees. It meant that you could have a career with Accenture but work for organisations such as CARE, Oxfam, the World Bank, the UN Development Programme… periodically for 3 to 6 months, not as a sabbatical but as part of your career with set deliverables and performance monitoring. Our idea challenged the norm where you graduate, leave the university gates and turn either towards the money grabbing private sector, or a bleeding heart NGO to use the stereotypical descriptors; a binary choice. It went beyond any offering from other large corporations both in terms of options for employees, and getting professional support to the development sector. Within the context of traditional corporate interaction with social issues, this was revolutionary stuff.

Funding-wise it was a three-way contribution model with Accenture, the participants, and the NGO clients all contributing to the costs. It was a sustainable, scalable offering of high quality services to organisations that traditionally couldn't dream of having access to Accenture, in countries where there was no commercial market for Accenture services. This meant that again we could go beyond the limits of a traditional CSR programme that only offered pro bono resources when the sun shined, there was following

wind and a benevolent Chief Executive around.

Gathering support

Our next challenge was selling the idea into the top levels of the organisation. Inspired by my memories of that FT article I wrote a fictitious article dated six months hence. It described Vernon Ellis, International Chairman of Accenture, launching a new non-profit arm of the business at the World Economic Forum. I sent this off and he seemed to like it. I then returned from Macedonia and got together the eight colleagues who wanted to make this happen and together we produced a pack detailing everything you needed to know about what would become ADP (essential in that process were Heidi Strawson, Sarah Dodds and Robin Schofield). We then set about convincing the five heads of the UK business, they who 'owned' the people and the money, to sanction a formal feasibility study. To appeal to this senior group we knew we had to stick to talking about the business case rather than the 'nice for the world' CSR angle: 'Here's an innovative model which will help you attract, keep and develop great people, and it will be cost neutral to Accenture.' We picked them off one by one to get a kind of domino effect: the first ones we had an inkling would be supportive, and when we got to the forth and fifth who were a bit more hard-line it was a case of 'you don't want to be the odd one out'. We got their buy-in and it was on with the study.

Striking 'data gold'

The study gave us helpful data about the development sector, and it told us that our people would be willing to work on the other side of the world for half their salary. But the real gold came when we correlated those who wanted to participate against performance bands and found a strong link between our top performers and levels of interest. This was great, there was something about the cream of the people Accenture wanted to recruit, retain and develop, which made them want challenging and constructive career models like ADP. They were telling us that they weren't overly bothered about salary and share options, they wanted choices within their career that meant they could use their skills to have a tangible impact on the world.

This obviously impressed the leadership, who collectively had pretty much never had an employee come to them and say they'd work for a lower salary; they're used to fending people off who are saying 'you don't pay me enough, I'm off to a competitor'. In effect our model was showing the Accenture establishment a whole new context for thinking about Human Resources and our HR people have really taken it to their hearts and supported us throughout.

Pilot time

The next step was to do a pilot to see whether this would work in practice, but where to start was an issue. We had this business case but not much of an idea as to how to start, and looking back we were bloody naïve: 'We're offering world-class management consultancy at a fraction of normal rates, therefore NGOs and donors will be falling over themselves to bring us in'. In reality there wasn't an existing market for business skills in the development sector, and where consultants did exist they tended to have 30 years' experience working in water and sanitation or health issues in Sub-Saharan Africa. We had no track record, no credentials, no client references; most of our guys had never even been to the developing world on holiday, and now we were offering strategy skills and IT systems in these countries.

When we did find a way into client organisations it was always through an individual. We found a few creative, take-a-punt type of people who despite working in some fairly regimented, bureaucratic structures were willing to take risks. I think that's been a common theme; entrepreneur to entrepreneur getting

things going. If I had to single out one key individual it would be Mark Goldring, VSO's own CEO. Mark shared the vision and our passion for ADP and confirmed the important role that business skills could have in the developing world. He's been a coach, a critic and a mentor throughout and now serves on our board. Well, it's really been a pseudo Board to date – we gathered together a few Accenture Partners (deliberately one or two natural cynics) and also senior figures from the outside world like Mark from VSO and Peter Armstrong, CEO of OneWorld to give us a bit of a reality check within the development sector. Vernon Ellis played the role of Chairman and most importantly provided the necessary air cover while we got the embryonic organisation off the ground.

So we had a degree of buy-in from the NGOs, and overarching support from a Board, but at the same time we had to recruit Accenture staff to actually work on the first projects. It's one thing people answering the questionnaire and saying, 'Yeah, I'm really interested in this', and quite another to actually sign on the dotted line of a revised employee contract to say, 'I will accept you docking half my salary to go and do this stuff, and I'm confident that it won't negatively affect my career'. There had been nobody go through ADP at that stage so those who did sign up really were the pioneers, people like William Sceats, Natalie Tuchband and Alison Bradbury; these guys really didn't know whether they would ultimately be rewarded by the experience.

'Creeping' to now

In the end we got some great first clients in the development sector, and some great first recruits to go out and work. Those early projects were a success and gave us experience, references and credentials, and on the back of them we gained momentum. From a handful of projects and a few people in the first year, we grew to 20 or so projects in the second year, to where we are now where we have 40 to 50 people out in the field all around the world, all of them working within their professional skill set to deliver core Accenture services to the development sector. To be honest getting established from the pilot stage forward was pretty blurred. We got creeping commitment, there was no hard stop between the end of pilot and steady state. We just kept going, and grew, and no-one has stopped us yet! (in truth, everyone's actually been really supportive).

We now work in two ways: either directly with NGOs and charities, or with donor organisations. The NGOs and charities pay us a fraction of normal market rates and we build their capacity and their operations in developing countries; the donor community pay us to be the arms and legs to implement their programs with an NGO; so we provide the skills, the donor provides the money, and the NGO provides the development project. In the early days developing relationships with the sector was really interesting. They'd say 'You should be speaking to the fundraising people if you are from Accenture; the private sector cut the cheques'. I had to say, 'I don't have any money, and actually I want to talk about you maybe paying us.' It was a whole new conversation that I believe is part of the process of redefining how the private and voluntary sectors interact. And now increasingly, they ring us.

Difficult means innovative

Telling the story of our launch like this makes everything sound pretty straightforward and linear, but even now not a week goes by when we're not breaking a company policy or a rule or a norm, or having a fight with someone. But I think that this 'struggle' if you like, represents the very fact that what we're doing is powerful and different from our normal business. The fact is we don't dot every i and cross every t, follow every procedure, or plan and analyse everything as is the norm at Accenture. For ADP to have come this far and to continue to develop we need to be a little more entrepreneurial than that.

The story today

Many of our current projects are related to the tsunami; several charities and NGOs are suddenly ten times the size they were before the wave hit, so they need to scale up their resources, their back office processes, their HR processes... to handle all that money. We're working with: CARE on this very issue in Jakarta; Oxfam on Livelihoods in Sri Lanka; Plan International to replace the childbirth registration system that was lost also in Sri Lanka; UNDP on IT and logistics work in Aceh; and we're about to start with World Vision on a supply chain project.

Aside from the tsunami work are numerous other equally inspiring projects. We're developing an e-learning system in Kenya to train 27,000 nurses, a process which traditionally would cumulatively take 100 years but with our help it will happen in five. We're applying supply chain expertise, the same that we might provide to western supermarkets, to improve the distribution of resources such as tents and medical supplies in instances of humanitarian disaster. We're working in Jordan and Eastern Europe with the world's largest micro-finance NGO to develop their strategic planning. We're working across South America and Eastern

Europe to streamline and digitise child sponsorship systems. And we're working with the IFC (World Bank) to strengthen their capacity to support small business growth to be an economic engine for development. These are just a few of our projects but they should give you a flavour of what we do. It should also show how we literally are applying the same expertise that Accenture supplies day in day out to corporate clients; effectively extending the high performance agenda to the development sector.

Looking forward

Clients are becoming increasingly interested in longer term relationships in which we'd help them to transform their organisations. A lot of the large international development organisations in this country desperately need to transform; they're doing great stuff, but they have to evolve in the same way that the private sector has evolved over the last few years. There needs to be a greater emphasis on enterprise and market orientated approaches to poverty reduction. For instance, I think we can apply the lessons learnt around consolidation: ensuring several organisations aren't chasing the same money to do the same things; getting charities in the same field to share some of their infrastructure... these are things that changed in the business world a long time ago and could really help take development forward. That will also mean we might start working at a western HQ, which will be great because there are clearly people who would love to work for an NGO but can't go to Bangladesh for six months because they've got kids or other commitments at home. Now we'll be able to offer placements in cities like London, New York and Paris as well as out in the field (although the focus of our efforts will still remain 80% in the developing world where there's the greatest need for our services but the least access).

Another exciting area for us going forward is making connections between Accenture's large commercial clients and ADP's development clients. We're in a great position to broker board level partnerships between these two sectors to tackle development issues. For me, we occupy quite a unique space to push this area forward in the next three to five years, effectively 'joining the dots' on these large, global issues.

We're also currently going through a change of legal status so that we can avoid some of those more bureaucratic processes within Accenture that are set up for large multi million pound contracts. I want us to really have the best of both worlds; to have privileged access to all those company assets that mean we can go beyond what a traditional charity can achieve, but at the same time to be a bit more nimble than the company is as a whole. Changing status also means we'll be a bit more palatable for a client NGO as they'll be paying money into a registered charity, rather than to a £25 billion market cap organisation!

Inspired!

The impact that our people create on ADP programmes amazes me every day; they just seem to step up a gear. When you take well educated, bright, highly motivated people with real experience in the private sector and put them in this context incredible things happen. If they're writing a business plan for an HIV/ AIDS NGO in Sub-Saharan Africa, knowing they'll impact on that situation in the next five years, you find they're pretty engaged in making sure it's a good piece of work. When they're developing the skills of the next generation of leaders in communities hit by the tsunami... I mean how motivating is that? Universally participants are saying, 'This is the best project I've been on, and just about the best experience of my life.' And, unlike any other scheme they're not having to step off their career ladder to do it; it's part of their career. On the client's side, organisations are coming back and saying, 'Is everyone as good as the team you sent us? We've never seen people so motivated or results focused.'

Our one concern is that people who go on ADP have such incredible experiences that they 'go native'. If good performers leave the business as a result of their time with ADP we will be closed down before you can say 'knife and fork'. ADP should be glue for Accenture. Our story has to be: good performer, goes away, comes back re-energised and having developed their skills, and loyal to Accenture because they want to work with ADP again in the future. At the moment we're achieving this; we actually have higher retention rates than the main business, not to mention differentiating Accenture as a progressive employer. We are in fact delivering a real business benefit.

Back to the floor?

I don't go on the projects any longer, I had my turn in Macedonia and that was fantastic. I get teased by the team that I should go back to the floor, and I would dearly love to do some of the projects, but there's just too much to be done in terms of managing and developing our business. This isn't 'a stint' and it's not me 'doing my bit'; I think most of the management team are on one-way tickets. I don't know where it'll lead us or how ADP will evolve, but I'm staking a career on it, and I won't be going back to a standard Accenture role, but then maybe roles like mine may become more standard in the future. This thing gets into your blood, and as business increasingly goes beyond philanthropy I think we're all in for exciting times.

My top tips

"Surround yourself with a top team (everyday I should be thanking Angela, Chris, Louise, Matt and Zoe). Although it might sound like this has been about my influence, my greatest achievement was surrounding myself with people equally as passionate and as able as myself. A few of their names have been mentioned in the telling of this story, but many more people have played an essential role in the creation of ADP."

"Gamble; these things need someone to stake their career to make them happen. I took myself off the career ladder, I said I don't need promotion and I don't care whether you call me a Partner, Manager, whatever. I also took a significant salary reduction amounting over the years to somewhere around six figures (they paid me too much!), and that tends to get the attention of the leadership here. But in the end the risk paid off in terms of a promotion which I think recognises the efforts of the whole team."

"Get support from people throughout the company: while this has been driven by employees, it could not have been done without the leadership support. They broke down some of the obstacles, supported us, and gave us a chance to be successful. If we didn't have that leadership support from the highest level we would not be where we are now. Also essential has been unofficial support from people throughout the organisation who simply bought in to the idea; friendly faces in finance, IT, HR, facilities... their help proved so important to ADP getting off the ground. You always need help."

"People are interested in this stuff, so play on that. ADP catches people's imagination, it's what they want to talk about in the pub and tell their family about. Remember that this field really does it for people."

Ideas you can steal

Make it personal

Gib's initial route into the development world was through people rather than organisations; a few individuals within development agencies were willing to give him a chance. Personal relationships are always the way to go, especially when you're dealing with some of the more traditional elements of the voluntary or government sectors. Select your champion and then get them inspired so that they move their organisation for you.

Talk other people's language

When Gib needed to persuade the five UK business heads he knew exactly which messages to push. Stories of social entrepreneurship often have many different dimensions: ADP is cost neutral, it benefits Accenture in terms of employee recruitment, retention and satisfaction, it's an integrated career option, and of course it delivers impact for the world. Gib 'turned up' the stories around the business case for the leaders, but for staff he talked more about careers and social impact. He knew his story inside out and recognised which bits would inspire different stakeholders.

Engage those at the top

Right from the outset Gib took his idea to the Accenture leadership, meaning he had doors opened and a degree of sponsorship that made things happen. He was both gutsy and creative in the way he approached them, managing to engage them even when he only had 15 minutes on the phone.

Sometimes it costs

Starting something new can mean personal sacrifice. Gib took a pay cut and risked his career, and everyone who goes on ADP needs to be able to sustain themselves on a lower salary for a period of time. Your average Accenture consultant isn't exactly strapped for cash, but those of lesser means might need to consider creative ways to keep their heads above water if they're going to change the world. What we would say is that showing some personal sacrifice, and that doesn't have to be financial, will inspire and impress those you need to get support from; it did for Gib.

Jo Confino

The Guardian newspaper, Social and Community Affairs: The Guardian is owned by the Scott Trust, and therefore unlike other newspapers, places its values ahead of short-term financial targets. The Social and Community Affairs team exists to ensure those values are 'lived' throughout the organisation in a way that is in line with its editorial content.

Why he's here

By promoting social, ethical and environmental issues through company values, Jo has put corporate social responsibility (CSR) at the heart of the organisation. What he has created at the Guardian is the very welcome opposite of the 'bolt-on' culture that undermines much of the CSR world. His work is not limited to the Guardian 'doing its bit'; it filters through to every layer of the company and has become a key part of how the organisation is managed. Jo is also a great example of that particularly patient variety of entrepreneur who can innovate within the dynamics of a large and well established company. Add to all this the fact that the Guardian's 'Living Our Values' report is one of the best examples of social auditing we've ever come across, and you've got a pretty special story of social entrepreneurship within an organisation.

Who is Jo Confino?

Jo was born in 1961. He went to an independent school, studied Government at Essex University, and then completed a postgraduate diploma in Journalism at Cardiff University.

His first job was on the Western Evening Herald and Western Morning News in Plymouth as a general reporter. He became the Business Correspondent for three years, and then moved to the Portsmouth News in a similar position.

Three months later he got a job on the Daily Telegraph where he spent three years as News Editor of the Business and Finance section, and three years as Wall Street correspondent in New York.

Jo then moved to the Guardian and for six years was the News Editor of the Business section. He is now an Executive Editor, Head of Social and Community Affairs for Guardian Newspapers Ltd, and advisor on corporate social responsibility to the Guardian Media Group.

The issues he confronted

The Guardian was founded in 1821 at a time of great social and political upheaval. Democracy and literacy were spreading, and the Guardian was founded to provide information so that people could become active citizens, and to make society more equitable.

CP Scott, who edited the paper from 1872 for 57 years, laid down the company values in his 1921 centenary leader article: 'honesty, cleanness [integrity], courage, fairness, a sense of duty to the reader and the community'.

The Guardian since 1936 has been owned by the Scott Trust, which places its mission to publish quality papers, free from party affiliation, remaining faithful to the liberal tradition ahead of financial returns. This gives the Guardian a freedom that is unique in the British newspaper industry

In the last 15 years Guardian Newspapers Ltd has grown significantly with the acquisition of the Observer and the launch of Guardian Unlimited. It has also moved into new areas of media such as films, books, television and online curriculum resources. This growth has meant that the values could not be maintained simply through the traditional method of osmosis between staff.

The solution he created

Jo formed a Society and Community Affairs team which focuses on reconnecting the whole organisation with the values of the Scott Trust. They have just published their third annual report 'Living Our Values'. Last year's report won a Clarion Award for 'effective communications that promote corporate social responsibility'. The report has been the catalyst for numerous changes throughout the organisation.

His team also co-ordinates a number of projects around the world relating to education, journalism and HIV/AIDS. Although some of the projects, such as community volunteering, sound like standard corporate social responsibility fare, they are leading edge and highly impactful.

Jo's story

The thing about values

Something that I find fascinating about my organisation is how the original vision and purpose has survived through 183 years and numerous management changes. It's so easy for these to be corrupted, or tainted, or forgotten over time, but they are absolutely vital to an organisation staying true.

I'm passionate about the Guardian and about journalism in general; I know it sounds trite to say, but if citizens are not informed society will suffer. I went into journalism with that lovely naïve belief that I could really make a difference. I'm still trying to hold onto that.

Because papers like the Guardian continue to hold an important role in fostering a healthy democracy by mediating the news and debate, it is essential that we have integrity in our editorial content and our business practices. Most people tend to think of the Guardian solely as a newspaper but forget that we are also a company of 1,500 staff covering everything from advertising, marketing, IT support, accountants and catering staff.

Living the values

The daily rush to produce newspapers means that it is easy to always concentrate on the here and now rather than for departments to think more broadly about their responsibilities.

What I've done is to focus attention on our corporate behaviour, and to help managers across the organisation to recognise that everyone needs equally to buy into and live the values. In a nutshell it's about practising what we preach.

It's simply not good enough to exhort our readers to take a course of action if we, as a company, are doing the opposite. For example, we probably take a stronger line on environmental issues than any other paper, yet until a few years ago we had not been following our own advice. Our environment correspondents were embarrassed to bring visitors into our building because of the chasm between our editorial coverage and our own behaviour. As individuals, as companies, as societies, if what we project externally is different from how we are behaving internally, at some point that will create stress and something will have to give.

The reason I moved from being a pure journalist was because I recognised there was a danger of losing touch with our values as we grew to be a much more diverse media business. The launch of Guardian Unlimited and various other new sections and supplements meant that there were hundreds of new employees who did not necessarily have a strong feel for, or an intimate knowledge of, our values. In editorial, for example, the old method of maintaining the values – junior reporter sitting next to senior reporter - wasn't working effectively anymore. Plus nobody had ever asked why the values were being talked about at the editors' morning conferences but not at, for instance, meetings in the building services department. So, I got the agreement of the editor that I should spend time bringing the values back onto centre stage, making sure that they resonated across the entire organisation, and had practical manifestations in everything we did.

And my story...

I tend to believe that what we are engaged in externally has a resonance with what we are seeking to do internally. So I recognised that my desire for the Guardian to be true to itself was also what I, as an individual, was also seeking to achieve.

At the time I was a financial journalist in the middle of my career and was starting to feel trapped.

It didn't seem all that obvious at the time but there was this great change happening within me, and it's only with hindsight that I recognise what experiences and events led me to this path.

One was a period of therapeutic work that was all about understanding my place in the world; all the stuff where you say 'yes I have value, I am loveable, I have got something to contribute...' I was good at my job and I lived a pretty full and busy life, but there was a part of me that I wasn't really projecting into the world. I was hiding away from the part of myself I disliked – places where I felt shamed, fearful and powerless. By jumping into my own abyss and facing these feelings, it helped me to understand how other individuals, groups or companies could transform their old patterns and beliefs. In other words, change was possible but only if one faced into the really scary places, rather than try to ignore them or skirt round them.

The other thing that I did was go on this little two day management training course for journalists, a rare thing because journalists hate to think of themselves as managers.

One of the key messages was that as managers we have a responsibility to spot problems and actually take responsibility for doing something practical about them.

To anyone else that's probably the most obvious thing in the world, but as a journalist it had genuinely never occurred to me before. I had always thought my responsibility was pages, not people. It wasn't an 'oh my god, I've seen the light' moment, but I did clock it and kind of stored it away in my head.

A little while later I had what I can only describe as a sort of epiphany; I can't explain it intellectually, but I came in to work one Monday morning and I just knew that there was something else I needed to be doing at the paper. I really felt like my life turned on a sixpence. Suddenly I recognised I could be an agent of change; I just had this deep-seated feeling that I could contribute in a bigger way.

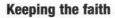

Keeping the faith

On that Monday morning I booked in to see the editor. He was very open towards what I had to say, and from that point on I just started to carve out a niche. It didn't all come at once, but the process got underway. The first thing I did was set up a community programme. Until the early sixties we'd been based in Manchester and were absolutely part of that community. We then came to London and moved into this 1960s office on Farringdon Road and were completely disconnected from anything and anyone local. So I set up a volunteering scheme with some local schools where our staff would go in and help with reading and mentoring. I know it sounds like box-ticking CSR stuff, but actually this had real meaning; not only did we help out the schools and give our staff a great experience, education is one of our big focus areas and this was a way for us to actually experience education. This scheme has now expanded to include other charities and organisations in the UK and Africa.

At the same time as setting up the volunteering programme, I came out of the business news department and took part in a two year process review of the company. It was essentially a change management programme; looking to develop processes that would help turn the company from being vertically organised to a more cross functional structure. The consultants who were helping us thought that it was pretty much a miracle that we produced the paper every day, and it must just be our passion that got us through.

You might think that a change management programme was somewhat off course after the 'drama' of my epiphany, but I learnt that it is not just good intentions that bring about change, but demonstrable and measureable actions.

The other great thing I learnt during this time was that just because I may have had some good ideas, it did not necessarily mean it was the right time to implement them. In other words I learnt to trust the ebbs and flows of the process. One of the recommendations of the process review was that we should carry out a social audit and that we should look at our values. I'd originally spoken to the Editor about it three years before, but the waiting was never a concern because I trusted that the time would need to be right in order to have broad support. In the meantime I had picked up some

fantastic learnings from the change programme: the internal dynamics of the organisation, what was lacking, where the opportunities were, and an overall faith that it is possible to create change even within an organisation as established as ours.

Starting properly

So three years after having had the idea, I got the go ahead to do a social audit. What was most important was for this to be a warts and all process and that it should be honest and transparent. The very last thing we were interested in was PR puffery and self-praise, which many CSR reports are about. Recognise our achievements – yes, but more importantly own up to our mistakes and create a process of constant improvement. To do this we did everything 'out loud' and externally facing. It's very difficult not to act on something when you make a public commitment.

To help us with this, we chose the toughest independent auditor we could find, one who didn't once mention the marketing opportunities associated with social auditing. So in the first year we set 40 targets right across all departments, and in the second year it was 54 and 29 in 2005/2006.

The blueprint for our social auditing journey was the approach I would have taken as a journalist. Ask the difficult questions, refuse to accept no for an answer, demand transparency and accountability, and go back and see what has changed.

The feedback to our reports has been fantastic. Every year thousands of copies are sent all over the world to newspapers, media organisations, journalism schools and those interested in CSR.

Corporate therapy...

One issue with social auditing is that it's a bit like going into therapy. As individuals, we love to be recognised for all our good qualities and hide all the negative qualities which we feel guilty about. The last thing we want is for these to be exposed because we are worried that we will be ostracised. For many people, it is only when they go into some form of therapeutic work, that they can start owning up to the stuff they feel mortified about and then seek to change what they are not happy about.

It's not so different for companies. They often have PR departments whose sole purpose is to project the good qualities of the company and to hide where things are going wrong so that they don't lose customers. This extends to CSR with most auditors and CSR professionals believing that 95% of social reports don't really address the core problems a company is facing. Organisations are scared of addressing their negative issues, but then so am I, so are you, we all are; who would chose to publicly expose all their wrong doing? Which company would chose to say 'OK we messed up, we're really sorry about that'.

...that does have an impact

But the fear of exposure is always worse than the reality because at the end of the day people know and respect when an individual or a company gets honest. Social auditing does work; the change we managed to drive within Guardian Newspapers Ltd through our audit is fantastic and so much more significant than your average CSR programme. In general terms, managers are now talking about the values, and they are truly top of the agenda. They are also being incorporated into managers' appraisals. In terms of change it's also been very effective; managers are actively engaging with the targets and meeting them. One of the areas of greatest change has come on the environmental front: previously we just purchased goods almost entirely based on price and quality; I went in and talked about values and they totally 'got it', and now virtually everything has changed or is changing: we're moving from using only fossil fuels to building our own wind turbines; we've increased our recycling by 300%; we've reduced our waste to landfill by 20%... A few years ago we didn't even have an environmental policy, now we've got a policy, a board champion and a steering group. It wasn't that people didn't care before, it just wasn't on their minds and we had no mechanism to put it there; this is how effective CSR can be if it's done in a meaningful way.

We've had similar levels of success in other areas: we didn't previously know how long it took to pay our suppliers, now we have a supplier survey and charter. We carried out our first employee survey in 2003 and the HR department has done a great job in addressing the concerns of staff, ranging from making pay and rewards more transparent, to improving learning and development.

It's all about connection

Apart from the social audit, I manage or have helped create several other projects. On the surface these can seem disparate and this has sometimes drawn comments from colleagues such as 'what the hell is your job?'.

But I've always been very clear that they all share a core theme around the issue of connection. There is too much separation in the world and too many barriers in our lives; every scheme is about connecting people to something meaningful. The community programme allows people who might be in the office all day to participate in society, something we've always encouraged our readers to do. The audit is about connecting the teams behind the Guardian, the Observer and Guardian Unlimited very clearly and consciously to the values. I also manage the Christmas appeal where we raise hundreds of thousands of pounds for UK and overseas charities. We have five weeks' coverage in the paper to drive the appeal, meaning it's not just about raising cash, but more importantly, an opportunity to really connect readers to the issue and get them fully engaged. We've set up a section on our website called 'Get Involved' where we connect readers with projects in Malawi and Ghana. We also set up a series of staff events, language classes, yoga, a choir...

so as to connect people from across the organisation no matter what department or level of seniority. Now they sing together, learn together, meet socially together. Everything I do here is about connecting people and bridging gaps between where we are and where we should be, and that's all it is.

Getting wider

Guardian Newspapers is part of a much bigger organisation of media businesses called Guardian Media Group (GMG) that includes regional and local newspapers, radio and the Autotrader stable of magazines and websites. The other companies are there to support the Guardian financially; they basically exist to make sure that the Guardian prospers.

There is a danger in this, of course, that the Guardian is able to live its values by forcing the other divisions in the group to be solely profit maximising.

But more recently there has been a much more conscious understanding that the Scott Trust values should apply to all the businesses it owns and that it makes no sense to be selective.

As a result, all the divisions within GMG are now going through their own social auditing process, although they are being given the freedom to translate the values for their own particular business.

Going further

This has to be a very dynamic process, and there is only purpose in me being here while it continues to bring about change. If I ever came up against a wall which there was no way around, or I ever get the sense that we are becoming one of those CSR teams that is peripheral to the organisation's core, I wouldn't do the job anymore. If I'm honest I think that so far we've gone for a lot of low lying fruit, you could say easy wins, but this is because there were issues that we couldn't ignore at the start.

But as we get deeper into the process, the issues become more complex and at the same time more subtle. I believe the next stage is about dealing with our culture. This is a difficult area because it is where companies often have a blind spot.

The Guardian's editor has often talked about the duality of being owned by a trust: it allows us extraordinary freedom to be innovative and to try things out, but at the same time the protection it offers us can strengthen the status quo; 'We've got the whole of the Guardian Media Group giving us money so why do we need to change?'. That's obviously not a conscious arrogance, but something that does unavoidably emerge in the background when you're supported in perpetuity.

My top tips

"The first thing I learnt more than anything else is to have courage; if you are withdrawn or you don't engage, then change will never happen. If I had not found the courage within me, I would not be doing what I'm doing now."

"Trusting the process is critical. However enthusiastic, ambitious, and confident you are of anything, that is not always enough on its own. You cannot force through change just because you feel sure of the outcome. It might take time, perhaps more than one attempt, perhaps gaining the support of other people, and it might need to lay dormant for a while, but keep the faith and it will happen."

"If you get people feeling connected to a purpose and understanding of their contribution, you'll get great loyalty."

"Be open to being wrong or to finding a better way; being true to your vision doesn't mean you know the best way of getting there. In other words don't stay hooked on the destination, but pay attention to the journey."

"In an established company you need to be an expert on influencing and getting people onside. That's about effective communication."

"The other point that's important to remember is that sometimes you need to be an outsider in an organisation to get change to happen. That can often mean that you don't immediately get the acknowledgement or recognition for what you are doing."

Call to arms

"Transparency is key if things are to improve. I'd call on all institutions, companies, government, NGOs to be transparent and to be honest, to do what they ask other people to do, and to own up to mistakes rather than trying to cover them up. If you continually try to cover things up so much gets distorted."

"At the same time we need to get rid of the idea that being honest will lead to judgement and guilt, otherwise society will shrink. The fear of being exposed is far greater than the reality."

Ideas you can steal

Make values something you can use

Most companies now have a declared list of values, even some pop stars have them. This is all good as long as they are not just general positive things that everyone would want to be. Values should be things that you fully understand, fully feel, that you call upon to help you through difficult situations; they should border on being a set of behaviours. Plus, they need structures to help you live by them. In Jo's case this is the social audit and the targets that are set there. That audit brings the values down from a lofty position to a set of clear actions that people at the Guardian can follow.

Social auditing is a tool not a brochure

Too many social reports just report, they don't initiate change. Jo was determined that his social audit should be a tool right from the start. If you don't follow this principle not only does it undermine the ethos of what social responsibility is all about, you'll also just get a very expensive brochure.

If you want something to happen, tell someone about it

Jo's 'out loud' theory is a great way to create momentum for anything that you think might be likely to stand still. Whether it's a launch, changes within an organisation, or something that you personally want to achieve, setting public targets will mean you're committed and far more likely to get on with it.

Be patient when creating change within an organisation

There are different breeds of entrepreneur, some that need to be outside and on their own, some that work more slowly and tactically within organisations. Jo is obviously the latter, he showed three years' worth of patience. Getting people to understand your idea and buy into it is difficult, and sometimes you need to be pretty calculated about what you ask for, when you ask, and who you ask. Be patient and be clever.

Get to know your organisation inside out

Creating change within an organisation demands that you know exactly how it works; its dynamics, its opportunities, its culture. Jo really got a thorough grounding in all these elements of the Guardian when he took part in the change management programme. If you're thinking of creating change within your organisation look for similar opportunities to get under the skin of how the place works and it will really tool you up to make those changes.

Sir Bob Geldof

'Pop star, poet, open-plan politician, living saint and self-confessed big mouth gob shite'. Bob's many achievements include Live Aid in 1985, the Drop the Debt Campaign, and Live 8 in 2005.

Why he's here...

To us, and probably most of world, Bob is a bit of a hero. Over the last 20 years he has pretty much single-handedly kept the world engaged and informed of the issues facing Africa through his concerts and campaigns. Since Live Aid, Third World debt has become a household concern and trade justice is a familiar issue to us all. Of Bob's many attributes, what we particularly admire is his ability to both make the world's most powerful political figures sit up and take notice, while at the same time bringing complex political issues to the masses.

?WHAT IF! UnLtd*

Who is Bob Geldof?

- Robert Frederick Zenon Geldof was born in Ireland on the 5th October 1951. Bob's mother died when he was 7 and he left school at 10 and worked as a factory hand and labourer. His first involvement in local politics came when he set up local CND and anti-apartheid groups.

- Bob's first love was music in which he had a hugely successful career. He was lead singer of the Boomtown Rats before going on to become a solo artist.

- Bob is a devoted family man and lives with his four daughters and his partner Jeanne. After having to fight for custody of his children he is also a campaigner for fathers' rights.

- Bob was awarded an honorary knighthood by the Queen in 1984, and he received the 2005 Man of Peace Award for his 'outstanding contribution to social justice'.

The issues he confronted

- In the early 1980s a drought in Ethiopia wiped out harvests, causing a devastating famine and threatening the lives of millions of people. Africa was at the time a 'forgotten' continent and Western governments were slow to get involved; aid to Ethiopia was lower than to most other developing countries.

- Ethiopia is also one of the world's poorest countries; almost half of its population live well below the poverty line and around 7 million Ethiopians can't produce enough food for themselves. Recurring droughts over the past 30 years, violent changes in government and conflicts with neighbouring countries have added to the instability and poverty. The average Ethiopian now lives on a pitiful $0.25 a day.

- Across Africa, many countries have spent more on debt than either health or education; Africa's total external debt is around $300 billion.

The solutions he created

- In 1984 Bob began his campaign to provide aid to famine stricken Ethiopia. He teamed up with musician Midge Ure to raise over £100 million through the Live Aid concerts in the UK and the States, and sales of the Band Aid single, Do They Know It's Christmas? In July 2005 he launched Live 8 to put pressure on world leaders at the 2005 G8 Summit. Bob is a staunch advocator for the Drop the Debt campaign which lobbies for 100% cancellation of unpayable and unfair poor countries' debts.

- Africa has since received unparalleled global attention; leaders at the Gleneagles Summit pledged to double aid to the continent by 2008. The Drop the Debt campaign has led to the UK promising to pay 100% of its share of the debt service being paid by poor countries to some multilateral institutions, for 10 years.

Bob's story

It's not Freud

People always try and relate to me and explain my life by referring to my childhood. I lost my mother when I was only seven very unexpectedly and yes, it did change my life and yes, it has had a profound affect on me but I would never say that I had a bad childhood. We grew up in Dublin in the 1950s and 1960s and Ireland was a hard place to live in then. My dad worked very hard as a travelling salesman and so was away a lot and my sisters were a great deal older than me and so I did spend a lot of time on my own. However, I sorted myself out everyday and although I may never have been the smartest boy at school I got myself there watered and fed everyday, well until I was about ten, when I decided school wasn't for me.

I guess in some ways my childhood prepared me for life at an early stage. I learned to be organised and take control of my life, although maybe to an extreme. I guess my independence had a dogmatic element to it in the end. If no-one is around you do become independent but then you also never have anyone to tell you that you're wrong or to take a step back. That can be an advantage sometimes but at other times people just think that you're an arsehole.

Mixing business with pleasure

Music was my first passion and is still the thing that drives me more than anything else. I worked on a few music magazines before we finally formed the band back in Dublin. The Boomtown Rats was an amazing time in my life and I loved it. There is something about getting on stage and having people appreciate you for something that you love; and to be able to combine music with the issues and politics that I believed in was also fantastic. I was lucky that I came of age when music and politics were so intertwined. I really do feel that music is what I must do and politics is what I have to do.

The rallying cry

When I realised what was going on in Ethiopia and the extent of the devastation I realised that I was in a great position to do something about it, and so I did. Midge Ure and I got all the bands and musicians together we could think of for Band Aid and we brought out the single 'Do They Know It's Christmas?' So many different artists came together to produce something that was really important and meaningful and really did make a difference - everyone in the country made a difference. The Live Aid concerts were great as well. The single was good as a means of raising money from British people but the concerts raised awareness on a global scale and hopefully served to keep the attention and focus on the issues in the long term. We raised over £108 million pounds for the famine victims in Africa. I was impressed and in awe of everybody for coming together like that. And that's a fucking load of money, it made a massive difference.

Balancing the books

The thing is I still had to have a business head on. Despite the fact that everybody was trying to do this great thing for charity, I had to make sure the money was going where it was meant to. I had the foresight to gain financial control of every aspect of the record production, manufacture and distribution so that it couldn't get swallowed up in royalties and administration. I managed to ensure that the famine relief programme received over 96 pence

from every record that was sold for £1.35, which is pretty good. Live Aid became my job, more than that, my vocation over the next three or four years. I gave up the band and focused on this. From 1984 until 1987 I only worked for Live Aid without any salary; we wanted every penny to reach Africa. I was lucky that I was in a position where I was able to do that for a while. Although by 1987 it was getting hard to devote myself entirely to the cause. I was still a part of it but I needed to take a step back - but like I said before, that's hard to do.

The thing was I had created this and I wanted to make it succeed, like anybody that embarks upon a project that they believe in. I had to build up a great deal of knowledge about what was going on in Africa and around the world; in particular about the social and political agendas of individuals and politicians and how that impacted on what was going on. I had to build up close working relationships with people, such as politicians, which I definitely wouldn't have done otherwise. I had to think about strategies and how to appeal to the maximum amount of people possible so that we could achieve the great thing that we did.

Rewriting history

I have now been working on Africa for 20 years. It is definitely an ongoing thing and even though I had a break after the initial furore diminished it was still in my mind and I was still constantly aware of what was going on there. That is why when the G8 Summit came up in July 2005 I realised that it was time to start again. There was a need to reawaken the project that I had started. However I never wanted it to be seen as Live Aid 2. It was a different issue but one that could be helped with a similar response. Once again I saw something that could be changed and that needed to be changed and I thought that it was my duty to do something about it. I had to come up with new and innovative ideas to try and win over and encourage as many people as possible and I had to have a lot of conversations and negotiations with Tony Blair and senior politicians. I know a lot of people looked on me unfavourably over that but he was the man that was going to be at the summit and making the decisions. I needed him to be onside.

Yes, I think that there is a willingness to change amongst a lot of people but there are always excuses on a lot of levels. Politicians are always claiming that the IMF is nearly bankrupt and that is why we can't give debt relief to poor countries. That's a load of crap and they know it. I just have to keep on and raise awareness that they are talking crap. How can you possibly expect a country to pay back money it doesn't have and that it needs desperately just to get simple basic healthcare? It's fucked up. That's why this is so important.

Getting angry and doing something about it

If I hadn't believed in Live Aid or Live 8 and been so passionate about it, it would never have worked out and become successful. That is the most important factor in anything that I do. I need to believe in it and be driven by it otherwise it won't work. My other business ventures may not have been inspired by such a pressing and important need as Africa but they've still been borne out of things that I have seen and thought, 'this is shit let's try and sort it out'.

An example of that is Planet 24 which I started up in 1992 with some close associates, Charlie Parsons and Waheed Ali. We decided to start making programmes that weren't completely crap, like so much of what was on the box at the time. We looked at the general output of television production companies and thought we could do better. So we did. We revolutionised morning TV for a start, with The Big Breakfast. That was great because it was just so different from anything else that was on and it wasn't boring. Our programmes were innovative and diverse and that is why they worked. The Word was also a great success and started the trend for rowdy, fun, Friday night TV But we also had more serious output that revolved around political commentary and documentary and we tackled a very contemporary and increasingly important issue by introducing Gaytime TV.

Deckchair.com started because I was trying to book a holiday to Disneyland for my family and it was so difficult. I rang lots of different travel agencies and they all gave me different ridiculously expensive quotes. I just thought that a regular family would get really pissed off with this, just like I did, especially as you could get cheaper flights if you looked hard enough. So I developed a site where you could book directly with the airlines cheaply and easily and then you get your ticket through the post. Easy. As with a lot of things with me I just get irritated when things aren't being done as they should and I try to change them. Deckchair.com was a success but I also sold it at a good time. I had to take stock of the current situation with .com companies and realise that they weren't doing that well. In 2001/2002 the internet shares were dropping and the internet booking phenomenon just wasn't taking off like it is now. So I sold it and I did well. To be honest this was something that I felt was initially really important and I felt the need to create a solution to holiday bookings, but when I realised the market just wasn't there at the time, I was happy to sell.

Ten Alps Production Is what I am involved with now and I founded this with Alex Connock and Des Shaw, again people that I know and trust. It is a development of Planet 24, and represents the same desire to produce high quality diverse programmes. We took on board the current interest in factual TV and have produced some really good programmes that have been popular, diverse and inspiring. We also produced some high profile documentaries that have been aired on the BBC, Channel 4 and the Discovery channel. If I can't produce good quality television programmes then there is no point in doing this, so it's important that we check our standards and quality all the time. I don't want the production company that I'm involved with to become as irritating and mundane as the ones that drove me to create this in the first place.

Going my own way

To be honest, I'm not a natural or conventional businessman. I do things in my own way but that's how I get things done. I don't have an office and I hate emails. I sort out my own affairs and don't expect a secretary or PA to do it for me; I think that's fair enough. I may appear a little disorganised but it works for me. I hold a lot of my meetings in a café on Kings Road; I find it a lot easier and far more comfortable than a stuffy office.

Going all the way

I have done well by getting pissed off about something, having an idea, doing something about it and taking it all the way until I sort it out. Once I have done that I am finished with it and I move on.

With Deckchair.com that was an easy goal to accomplish. However with something like the Drop the Debt campaign it doesn't get sorted that quickly and you have to devote yourself to it in a larger more involved way. That's fine for me; I want to take it all the way until there's literally nothing more I can do.

Ideas you can steal

Use your anger constructively

Bob is in his element when taking something he hates and turning it around. That's the mark of a great social entrepreneur: they're always on the look out for solutions to things that annoy them, and they won't let things lie until they're resolved. And for Bob, it seems that's a never-ending quest. But if you can take just one thing that really gets your goat and commit to changing it for the better, you're on to a winner.

Do your homework

Over the years Bob has amassed a huge body of knowledge on Africa and third world debt, which is one of the reasons he is taken so seriously in politics. It might sound obvious, but it's essential that you know your subject inside out. If you can speak with utter confidence about issues that you want to tackle you're much more likely to get a captive audience.

Go with what works for you

Bob has his own inimitable way of doing business; he's persistent, he's single-minded, and he's disorganised, but it works for him. Why change something if it ain't broke. Recognise how you work best, warts and all, and stick with it; it's probably better than trying to do things in the conventional way.

Know when to move on

Sometimes it's a good idea to take a step back and have an objective look at where you are. This will help you decide whether it's time to move on or change direction; if you're too emotionally involved in the everyday stuff it can be harder to make a smart move. Bob is clearly emotionally involved in everything he does, but when it came to selling deckchair.com, he took stock of the situation and made a clear-cut business decision.

Matt Scott

Cosmos Ignite Innovations: a company, now based in India, trying to bring empowering products to the world's poorest people. Their first product is a solar powered lamp to replace the use of unhealthy and expensive kerosene lighting.

Why he's here

Matt's team have designed a light that could quite literally save millions of lives; that would be reason enough to include his story, but our interest really lies in the fact that his aim is to distribute his product by bringing it to market. 'Trading rather that giving' is a fundamental tenet of social enterprise, and to our mind it represents the most exciting of revolutions in the development world. Seeing how Cosmos Ignite is navigating the issues of trading with some of the world's poorest people is fascinating stuff. Also interesting is the fact that Cosmos Ignite Innovations is in its infancy, so unlike our other stories, it gives us a glimpse of what it's like for a social entrepreneur in the early days; how to scale up to bring prices down, how to survive Indian wages when you live in the UK… and what you do after your first big success.

?WHAT IF! UnLtd*

Who is Matt Scott?

- Matt was born and brought up in Wolverhampton in the Midlands, and studied Physics at Manchester University.

- He graduated to work in the science industry with AEA Technology. In his five years there he focused on a change management programme to inspire innovation and entrepreneurship within the company which had recently been privatised. He also worked extensively in risk management consultancy.

- Matt then earned a Fulbright Scholarship to study at Stanford Business School in California; Ignite's birthplace. After graduating he spent two years between both the US and India working on Ignite, and now lives in south-west London.

The issues he confronted

- 4 billion people earn less than $4 a day, 1 billion of whom live on less than $1 a day.

- 1.6 billion people, that's five times the population of Europe, don't have access to electricity, and a further 1 billion only have sporadic access.

- Most of these people use fuel-based lighting such as kerosene lamps. These lamps contribute to indoor air pollution, the world's second highest cause of premature death after water-related illnesses. They also cause accidental fires and burns and emit millions of tonnes of CO_2 every year.

- Expenditure on kerosene often accounts for more than 10% of a person's annual income, and can cost up to $10 per month.

The solution he created

- The light is solar powered, clean, safe and very hardy, and a day's charge will easily allow it to light a room for a family's whole evening. It uses new light-emitting diode (LED) technology to significantly increase efficiency and brightness compared to conventional incandescent bulbs or kerosene.

- At the moment the light's price is $50, including the solar panel. This is already far less than traditional solar home systems and as manufacturing volume increases and the technology improves, the price will go down – hopefully to $30 or less in future.

Matt's story

A beginner's guide

For me, the story started with my admission to Stanford, an incredible experience that opened my eyes to so many different things; I'd never heard of social entrepreneurship, I'd hardly even heard of entrepreneurship. Social and environmental issues had never been a huge driver for me, but at Stanford it all became exciting, and because I was on a scholarship I also felt exceptionally lucky; having had that opportunity I thought it would be fitting to put it to some worldly use.

In my first year I did a class on social entrepreneurship, learning about new exciting models for social change such as the Grameen Bank which gives loans to the poor in Asia, TransFair which deals in Fair Trade coffee, and several inspiring Ashoka Fellows (Ashoka is an institute for social entrepreneurs). These people would come and present to us, and the thing that gripped me from the start was that these projects were being done in a really entrepreneurial, business type of way while at the same time delivering tremendous social impact.

In my second year I took another course very descriptively titled Social Entrepreneurship Start-Up. It was a pretty intense class and came along when I was struggling with an already full final year workload, but I'd caught the social entrepreneurial bug and just went for it. There were about 20 students from across disciplines; business, engineering and design, and the whole aim of the course was to try and find a replacement for kerosene lighting in the developing world. The engineers and designers would work on the technologies and the product design; whether it should it be solar powered, water powered, wind-up, how we'd store the energy, the sort of light source we'd have… At the same time, the business school students worked on making the project sustainable – for example, researching how much people are already spending on kerosene, the different distribution options, the varying business models… So, there was a big mix of things going on, and

I was sitting on what they called the global team that tried to pull everything together.

The science bit

To get techy for a moment, we were taking advantage of new developments in LEDs. Basically traditional incandescent bulbs act more like heaters than lights; they give off 95% heat and, by the way a bit of light too. An LED is the opposite; it gives 95% light and 5% heat, and therefore requires much less power to produce the same amount of light. What's also exciting is that LED technology is rapidly improving, so our product will only get better.

The business bit

Fairly early on we decided that the business case had to be sustainable and target the emerging segment known as the 'base of the pyramid' A quick explanation: there are 4 billion people, that's most of the world, living on less than $4 a day. That means that there is a huge social need out there, but also a huge market for the right products at the right price; a guy called CK Prahalad has described this as the 'fortune at the base of the pyramid'. At the moment the market at the bottom of the pyramid is largely untapped. Our project focused on creating a product that would meet the needs of the 1.6 billion people without electricity. The theory (that I passionately believe in) goes that trading with the base of the pyramid can have a longer lasting, more sustainable impact than just providing poor people with charity: even with very generous support there will always be a limit to how many people you can serve with charity; in addition, giving to people doesn't encourage empowerment and can lead to them becoming dependent; giving can also interfere with local markets and prevent natural economic growth; and, there's always that risk that when you give rather than trade, people don't value the goods.

Our aim was to design something that was cheap enough that we could successfully trade at the base of the pyramid, and because people already spend money on kerosene there's a real opportunity to provide an economic, as well as social alternative.

Going for the Holy Grail

The course was a very intense experience and we finished after 10 weeks with a solar-powered light and huge momentum behind what we were doing. Because it was the first time it had ever run nobody really knew what to do with that momentum. I don't think anybody expected that the outcome would be a fully-fledged business; I certainly didn't as I'd actually signed up for a consulting job back in the UK! But when the time came a few of us just felt so excited that we were compelled to continue. A team of people went out to India with some prototypes and worked with NGOs to test them in the field. Unfortunately I got to stay at home and work on the business plan! We had to see if the theory would hold true, and if the product we'd designed could really transform people's lives as it was intended.

The experience of the team in India provided enough incentive for us to keep the momentum going, although there were a few fundamental decisions to be made. The end of the course had brought with it a strange kind of vacuum with no clear direction - there was us the group of students and our vision to create a sustainable business serving the world's poor, there were some members of the university who wanted to keep it as an academic project, and then there was the foundation that we'd been working with who had more of a philanthropic model and viewed our work as an extension of their own organisation. After a few tense conference calls (not for the first time!) we went ahead with our own vision: a profitable business that could change the world. That to us was the Holy Grail; something that makes money and becomes sustainable, while improving the lives of millions of people.

Money, money, money

That decision basically marked the formation of Ignite. There were three founders, all from the course, (one engineer and two business students) plus two other students who later became members of the team. We spent the first six months split into different roles: the engineers were working on the product, the other ex-business student went off to India to form manufacturing and distribution partnerships, and I was tasked with raising capital. It was challenging to manage everything in parallel between India and the US, and between getting the product ready and raising capital. It took me six months to secure our first significant investment and when it came it was a real breakthrough – from a guy called Vinod Khosla, one of Silicon Valley's leading venture capitalists. That cash allowed us to develop the product further and to pay ourselves some very minimal salaries to keep our heads above water. Having agreed a valuation for the company, we then went on to raise additional money from around five to ten more angel investors.

Our ambition was to get to a design that allowed us to retail the light at $25 to $30. However, we soon learned that there is a big difference between student research and the real experience of trying to make things happen, especially working in India for the first time. The deals on the components and materials just weren't there for us to take the price that low, and we also had to trade-off between the price point, how bright the light was, and how long it would last. For example, we probably could have produced a $30 light but it would not have lasted as long or be as bright as the current version – finding out what rural users in India really need is an interesting challenge! Our first product priced at $50, can last up to nine hours and be as much as 10 times brighter than kerosene; - the $50 price point is already a significant improvement over the larger scale solar systems that often retail for as much as $500. Finding the right balance between performance and price is a work in progress – within the 4 billion people at the 'base of the pyramid' there are many different segments. For example, somebody who is earning $4 a day is in a very different position from someone who's earning $1 a day. We've started by targeting those at the top of the base, and as the price drops we'll be able to reach more and more of those 4 billion people through a sustainable, business-based approach. At the same time, trading with the billion people at $1 a day or less will always be difficult, and there's clearly a role for a more traditional philanthropic approach. It's not the case of either/or – both trading and charity have important roles to play and combining the best elements of both will be very powerful. In the future, I'm confident we'll get down to a $30 price point through a mixture of re-engineering the product, building manufacturing volume, and taking advantage of improvements in technology.

Being a proper business

By consolidating our activities into a single Indian entity we've completed a rather inevitable transition from the continuation of a student project in California to a real business moving forward in India. Doing business in India is an incredible (and sometimes frustrating) experience – I've learned a ton! Thankfully we found a fantastic Indian partner with the insights, the local knowledge (and the patience!) to guide us through the tough times and keep us moving in the right direction. Our vision is now largely in our partner's capable hands, although we're doing everything we can to support the future growth - I'm confident Cosmos Ignite will become a great role model for future businesses and something we can all feel very proud of.

No champagne moment, but we're getting there

Unfortunately we never really had that milestone moment when we launched; although we've celebrated different moments along the way it's really been more of a gradual thing. We had these big bottles of champagne for the first order, but the first order is difficult to identify because you have samples, and then trials, and then tasters... these things don't have the big eureka moment. In reality launching a social enterprise in India is more a case of navigating your way through a series of problems. When we've sold a million lights, then I think I'll say 'Right, okay, we're on our way'.

So far we have around a thousand units going out to tsunami relief projects in southern India, we're also discussing sending lights to Pakistan as part of the earthquake disaster relief, and are part of a regeneration project in Afghanistan - now we have the product ready, the business is really beginning to take off. Obviously, the provision of light can be a huge benefit, especially at times of need such as the aftermath of natural disasters. As you can imagine being in the dark can be hugely debilitating, both physically and emotionally, and of course there are security implications; it's just very hard to do anything without light.

Beyond the NGO market we're keenly looking at commercial channels mainly in urban and semi-urban areas. In India, there's a vast network of dealers supplying a multitude of small shops all over the country – many of these shops sell a wide variety of products rather than being big branded electrical superstores like Currys in the UK. Targeting urban sales is important – many people at the base of the pyramid are increasingly migrating to cities; within the next 10 years there's estimated to be between 1.5 and 2 billion people living in the top 100 cities across the globe, with many of these being in the developing world.

Selling to the semi-urban and rural communities will probably mean linking up with microfinance groups. There are some amazing things going on in that world, like the Grameen Phone where basically one lady in a village is given a loan to buy a phone and then she rents it out to people in her village for calls; suddenly she has a profitable business, and the village is able to communicate with the outside world. It's about breaking things down into bite-sized chunks to make them affordable, and we're looking at a similar model where the light can be bought through microloans, rental schemes or other models of flexible purchasing that will increase our affordability by spreading up-front costs into smaller payments.

There's also a Western market for this, and that's kind of a work in progress for us. Over time, we could perhaps develop a model targeting campers, climbers, outdoor types and then use some of those profits to help bring our products to the developing world. It would also help us to increase our volumes and bring prices down. Perhaps serving the top and bottom of the pyramid is the best way to really make this happen?

Finding that personal balance

Cosmos Ignite is continuing to grow in India, and my role has now gone through a transition to one of Board Director rather than full-time employee. I feel very proud to have got the project to a point where it's in good hands in India, orders are coming in, and the company is sustainable and going forwards. I've now returned to the UK to find my next exciting challenge while supporting the future growth of Cosmos Ignite. One of the key questions is how I can stay involved with a business that is situated in the developing world and also support myself financially living in the UK. I'm confident I'll always have a lifelong connection to Ignite's work, at the same time, I also need to start paying some bills! I've also spent the last year flitting between India, the UK and the US, sleeping on people's floors and not having a home either personally or professionally - hence I'm finding it exciting to be back and looking forward to finding a little more stability and solid ground – at least for a while.

I think the dilemma of following your heart and your passions while balancing the financial realities of life is something many of today's younger generation are currently working their way through. On the one hand, with free flowing information and global travel we've never had as much opportunity – on the other hand, university debts and rising house prices present some very real financial obligations. It's all about finding the right balance – and everyone's different. Perhaps you find that balance by earning a lot of money as quickly as possible, and then pull out to fully engage in social entrepreneurship or follow your passions, perhaps you find a job that pays reasonably and allows you time to do other things, or perhaps there are jobs out there that have it all; an impact and a good pay packet? Ask me in a month!

My top tips

"Deals are never closed until the money's in the bank. It took six months from the first meeting to secure our lead investor. Pursue things like crazy, don't relax until they can't ask for it back, and just believe that it will happen in the end – confidence is contagious, and many people will be looking at you to set the example."

"Things take twice as long as you think and cost twice as much; and that's when things are going well! So if you add those things together you need four times more money than you first thought. Be patient; remain flexible in your approach and keep focused on the vision, it will work out in the end."

"Relationships are the oil that makes the machine run, so you need to get face-to-face contact as early as you can in a relationship. One of our big challenges was that India is 12 hours ahead of California, so we relied a lot on conference calling. We'd be in the middle of discussing a really tense issue and you'd realise the line had been dead for the last three minutes! If we'd all met face-to-face before those tough calls things would have been a hell of a lot easier."

"You will lose control along the way, and that's to be expected. Obviously always strive to do the right stuff, but there are so many different factors that you'll never keep it all in check. Do all that you can, but try not to worry too much about the destination, focus on enjoying the ride."

"Keep your eyes open because some opportunities are hard to spot. I met one of our investors on a plane; it's a bit of a cliché, but we went from having a chat to three months later him making an investment in our company. Now I just talk to everybody all the time because you never know who's going to make a connection."

My call to arms

"I want to connect with organisations interested in distributing the lights. We have the product now and it works well, we just need to get it out there."

"I also think UK companies, investors, and the man on the street could do more to encourage people to take risks. In Silicon Valley, venture capitalists tend to look for entrepreneurial scars as much as medals, because going through the entrepreneurial learning process is huge, whatever the result. When a venture does go wrong the attitude is 'good on you, you've learnt a lot, now put that experience to use'. I find the UK tends to be more risk-averse, putting a lot of emphasis on professional qualifications and brand names. This can often lead to people taking safer options and following more established career paths – I'd love to see more people step out and find their own path and for more recruiters to respect and support this."

Ideas you can steal

Go with momentum

Matt had made plans for his career after Stanford, but recognised that momentum was behind the light project both for him personally and in a wider context. Momentum is that magic energy that makes things happen; when you see it you grab it and go with the flow.

Know when to change your structure

Social ventures often have very complex structures that change quickly as the enterprise develops. They can change from charities to businesses to foundations governing for-profit enterprises... and like Matt's business, can start in one country and uproot to another as circumstances change. Matt was adept at recognising when things needed to change, and flexible enough to embrace those changes, even when it meant the venture would continue without him involved full-time.

You don't have to be a social entrepreneur for life

Matt went into social entrepreneurship because he was inspired at a certain time in his life, and now he might have a break until the conditions are right again. You don't have to 'jack it all in' for life, move to India and say goodbye to cars and holidays, and you don't need to commit for life to prove yourself worthy in this field; social entrepreneurship can be something that you engage with when it's right for you.

Sue Welland

The CarbonNeutral Company (formerly Future Forests): helps companies and individuals calculate the amount of carbon they are responsible for emitting, advises them on reduction, provides offset in the form of forestry or 'green' energy schemes, and helps companies to communicate their resulting CarbonNeutral® status.

Why she's here...

Sue and her business partner Dan Morrell took the most profound environmental problem of the modern era and developed an enterprise which totally changes the way we look at it. They translate climate change from being this huge intangible concern into being something that the man in the street can understand and take responsibility for. We think that Sue and Dan have shown a pretty unique level of understanding as to what it takes to move individuals and companies to change their behaviour, and that the principles of their model might just hold the key to alleviating some of the world's other intractable issues.

?WHAT IF! UnLtd*

Who is Sue Welland?

Sue was born in Midhurst, Sussex, but her family constantly moved around so she attended several different schools. That meant school years were a bit of a challenge, but she flourished academically and finished her education with a first class English degree from Sussex University.

Sue began her career in television working on sponsorship and production, moved to British Airways and then went to the PR agency, Charles Barker. One of her clients there was Eurotunnel whom she went to work for, in Paris for their launch.

She returned to the UK and became a freelancer working on a number of different projects from manufacturing to fireworks to property development to Future Forests. Sue got married in 2001, and had her first child in 2003 at the age of 42.

The issues she confronted

Climate change is caused by the release of greenhouse gases, primarily CO_2, which traps heat around the Earth causing global warming. Over the past 100 years the Earth's climate has warmed by about 0.6°C because of human activity, and this has caused rain and snowfall patterns to change, sea levels to rise and most non-polar glaciers to retreat.

Despite recent regulatory progress on climate change through the Kyoto Protocol and the European Union's Emissions Trading Scheme, emissions are actually growing at their fastest ever rate.

The only people trying to tackle climate change when Future Forests was launched were charities who focused on telling people about the problem rather than offering solutions.

The solution she and Dan created

The CarbonNeutral Company was launched in 1997 (then known as Future Forests). It offers both companies and individuals the chance to offset the carbon that they are responsible for producing, thus making them CarbonNeutral.

The offering is three-fold: calculating how much carbon a client is producing, advising how to reduce carbon emissions, offsetting unavoidable CO_2 through forestry and green energy projects, and communicating a client's CarbonNeutral status

The scope of The CarbonNeutral Company's work goes from strategic consultancy and carbon management for corporate and government clients, through to climate-related gifts available on the high street.

Sue's story

An entrepreneur from the start

I've always been entrepreneurial; embarrassingly, when I was at primary school I used to hire out my felt-tip pens so that people could colour in maps. I began my career in the corporate world, but that spirit, and an instinct of wanting to work for myself always stayed with me. In my early thirties I also became unhappy with the value systems of large corporations, and about applying my skills to projects which didn't have any long-term or real social integrity. I had a skill set which was around communications and how to package up an idea, I wanted to apply that to something which was more worthwhile than selling yet another airline seat, and to something that was driven by me.

I set up Future Forests in 1997 with a guy called Dan Morrell, it was Dan who originally had the idea. One day he was walking down the Hanger Lane and as always there was loads of traffic, but he noticed that the trees were wonderfully green and this made him think of his schoolboy biology; trees soak up CO_2 and put out oxygen. This triggered just the germ of an idea around packaging up gas exchange in a way that people could buy it. Dan and I were working together on a few other projects, and gradually, we started to work on the Future Forests idea and bring it to life.

No existing responsibility

It's important to set the scene a bit here. This was a time when climate change wasn't really on the agenda for consumers, let alone corporates, and the space was dominated by the environmental charities who do a great job but tended to focus on the negative; it's all about melting ice fields, burning rainforests… That stuff of course is happening, but it's not empowering, in fact it often just causes people to withdraw from the issues. So what Dan and I set about doing was to develop an idea which emphasized the thing about climate change which is both bad and good; we all cause global warming, so we can all do something about it.

What we wanted to do was to position tackling climate change in the same way as you would removing refuse from your house,

because it's the same thing; it's about recognising what you've produced and thus what you're responsible for. Our idea was to quantify the bit of climate change that you caused, and then create units of carbon offset in the form of trees (we only did trees back then), which you could buy to neutralise what you were responsible for. The beauty of the idea was in the tree: it satisfies a person's immediate desire to do something positive for the environment because you can see and feel a tree, but it also does a global good because biology makes it so; it does soak up CO_2 and give off O_2.

Making global warming bite-sized

Our idea allowed us to compartmentalise climate change issues into bite-size chunks, and that is a powerful message: this tree will soak up the tonne of CO_2 which you produced from, e.g. driving your car, over x period of time. We tell you where your tree is in the ground, and we give you a certificate to prove that you are now CarbonNeutral. What was new and unique was the sense of specific connection it created between individuals or companies and climate change.

Looking back it's difficult to see where 'the epiphany' was; I think an idea really grows by gradations, and I don't think you have a true idea until it's crystallised into a proposition that can be sold. That was what Dan and I brought to this project; the ability to be creative about how we packaged the idea so that people would buy it. For a long time we had lots of bits of paper describing something around creating forests at the same time as tackling climate change, but it didn't all come together until we had a packaged equation with trees planted equaling offset.

Just business

Early on we knew that to deliver this concept we shouldn't be a charity. To my mind charity is often about something that you didn't cause and you've got very little control over like AIDS or cancer. That's just not the situation with climate change. We do cause it and we can do something about it. We were more suited to being a business than a charity.

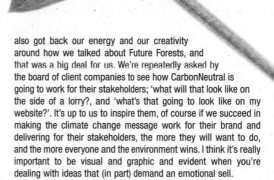

Getting the cash together

With the idea set we started looking for clients and we went to see an oil company called Greenergy about becoming CarbonNeutral. It was one of those weird meetings where you don't know where the dynamic's going; the guy was so interested in what we were saying that he soon veered away from sales talk and decided he was so excited that he wanted to buy into the company!

So our first piece of investment was pretty much unplanned. The Greenergy money set us up as a proper business and meant we could afford some desk space and a person to help us manage ourselves. That kept us going for a while, but there certainly wasn't much left over to pay Dan or I. We had mortgages and bills to pay, so for the first few years we carried on with day jobs and did Future Forests in the evening. As more work came in Future Forests became the thing that we were doing in our days and the other stuff happened in evenings to generate cash.

In 2000 venture capital (VC) money finally came in and we could both stop doing other work and focus entirely on Future Forests. I think what won over the venture capitalists was our very smart virtual delivery concept. It was at the time when Internet propositions were really booming and we had a system where people could pay for a tree online and then we delivered them a certificate; there was nothing like the complexities of online grocery shopping with packaging and thousands of products. The money meant we could really step-change the business; until that point we'd had to go pretty slowly when really we'd been wanting to cause a revolution. I think that's the point at which we knew we could create something significant in terms of corporate and consumer movement, and that was very exciting.

Beyond the trees and back to imagination

When we'd got tree dedications right we began to look at wider CarbonNeutral concepts; CarbonNeutral flights, CarbonNeutral homes… and suddenly things really began to open up. We took this to extremes in 2002 when we set about getting Newcastle to become a CarbonNeutral city. This was a really exciting project, not just because it took CarbonNeutral to a new scale, it also really reignited our creative drive for what we were doing. In the early days we used to say to people 'look how powerful this proposition is', and we'd get excited with how we told the story, and especially around images that we used to sell the idea. But as we'd got immersed in the business it had become a bit dry; lots of papers produced, lots of emails, and we sort of lost sight of the excitement of selling the creative vision. I think there's something there about how business, unchecked, can become about the most efficient way to do something, and that might be just getting a proposition down on paper.

With Newcastle we'd got into that rut using quite dry presentations and it was all moving very slowly. Then I got my husband involved (he's a creative director) to help us get back to images and creative ways of selling; 'this is what it might look like, you could have all of your trains dressed like this…' and suddenly the whole project started to move again and it was just fantastic. Within the year we had all sorts of exciting stuff happening. We also got back our energy and our creativity around how we talked about Future Forests, and that was a big deal for us. We're repeatedly asked by the board of client companies to see how CarbonNeutral is going to work for their stakeholders; 'what will that look like on the side of a lorry?', and 'what's that going to look like on my website?'. It's up to us to inspire them, of course if we succeed in making the climate change message work for their brand and delivering for their stakeholders, the more they will want to do, and the more everyone and the environment wins. I think it's really important to be visual and graphic and evident when you're dealing with ideas that (in part) demand an emotional sell.

Going corporate

Our first corporate sale was to Mazda, and what surprised us was the issue wasn't around them not 'getting' what we were about, it was that they would be the first company to raise their head above the parapet and say something about climate change. Their fear was that people aren't stupid and they associate cars with pollution; they might judge Mazda as being tokenistic. That's an interesting issue with corporates; it's not always about persuading them something is the right thing to do, it's about them being wary of cynicism when they do do the right thing. In the end we persuaded them to go for it and they made driving their fuel-efficient family car CarbonNeutral, and they made their company headquarters CarbonNeutral. It was a big deal for us because not only was it a large corporate, it was also a car company. We spent all of the Mazda money after the offset costs, on a PR campaign to help us with the messaging. That turned into a massive success for all sides; Mazda got £2.5m worth of coverage for the £50k they spent, and they had no negative feedback at all. Plus it gave us some great leverage to then go and sell to other companies.

Getting people connecting and finding evangelists

When we go into meetings with companies we say to them that they have the opportunity to change the world; it sounds a little cheesy, but it's an incredibly empowering message that excites people personally, and it's true. Obviously if you're the CEO you can change things pretty easily, but our contact at Avis who really championed Future Forests within that organisation was an account executive. She just seemed to get what we do so she helped us develop the proposals that were put in front of the UK marketing director; five years on and Avis are still with us.

That's one of the fantastic things about our company; people become determined about CarbonNeutral because it's such a simple idea which they can see working for their company and for the greater good. That's when it feels like a movement, when the people that become clients go on to become more than clients. It goes beyond them recommending us, they start to pursue and pursue and pursue their contacts to get in touch with us because they really believe it's the right thing to do. People connect with what is I suppose the essence of our idea and our brand in a very personal way, and they really want to see their friends and their company do the same thing.

The guys who work here are also connected to the spirit of what we're trying to do. That sounds a bit woolly jumper, but nobody's paid huge amounts of money, despite the fact that they all have commercial experience. At the bottom line they're choosing not to go somewhere better paid because they like the value of what we do over and above money. That isn't to say they wouldn't all love to be paid more, of course they would, but there is something else here that is exciting. Having said that we employ people who are commercial - I'd rather have cynics or sales people here who understand proposition development, marketing language, commercial pricing matrices... all of that stuff. We want people who want to develop this as a 'good business' not a green lobby. I want the NGOs to be around, but we add something which is a commercial twist, and which looks at it from the clients' side rather than just the side of environmental activism.

The connection appeal also extends to celebrity; we have several celebrity partnerships which is both a positive and a negative,

almost in equal measure. It's a massive positive because that kind of brand association and reach is like magic dust which goes beyond money. The only issue is that we have to be very determined to clarify with management and celebrities that we're doing a good thing, but that doesn't mean we're a charity, and we do more than trees. Sometimes messaging is a real challenge.

We were revolutionary; we're still unique

When we started we were revolutionary; people were talking about global warming, burning rainforests, melting ice caps... but they weren't giving people solutions. No-one was talking about carbon offset or equations or giving people small-scale solutions which were directly related to their contributions. There are now other organisations doing similar stuff, and that's great; competition means that when we talk to a company both sides have a benchmark, a point of comparison, and we're not talking in a foreign language. Where we are unique is in the length of time that we've been in the market, and the fact that we've done most things in the field. Where we excel is in our ability to navigate clients through issues that are very complex. No other company does everything from carbon consulting and risk management through to marketing communications. We may have competitors in each of those different areas but there's nobody who does the three-piece. It's that combination that is important; if you can understand all the front stuff, carbon consulting, offset and carbon reductions, then you can really add value to the marketing piece as well.

Over the course of the company's existence the market has become a lot more sophisticated; trees have fallen a bit out of fashion, and businesses have taken the issue of climate change much more seriously. We now help clients manage and reduce their carbon emissions, whereas before we were really talking just about offset. The way we offset is also changing increasingly towards technology as well as forestry offsets because it's a more effective way to address global warming. As a consequence we've changed our name from Future Forests to The CarbonNeutral Company. Future Forests was a loved brand because it was the first player in the market and we sold the very first offsets for consumers, but it also suggested that we were a bit of a niche, just dealing in forests so only a part of the problem, whereas actually we've been doing the total solution for some time now.

Our ambition is that CarbonNeutral will be the 'Intel Inside' of every product and service worldwide and there's no reason that it can't be. Carbon is instantly an international currency because everything can be counted in terms of carbon, and therefore you can ultimately hold somebody responsible for having produced it; therefore CarbonNeutral can be everywhere.

It's not about me

When you leave the corporate world to start a company there is a real step-change; you move from a secure salary and lots of people doing lots of things for you, to having no guaranteed income and you doing everything yourself. That means you become incredibly personally involved. After I had a child I was supposed to only work three days a week but I actually work seven days, and my percentage of the company is in fact now tiny because of all the rounds of VC money we've had in; I still feel so inspired by the idea, and so committed to the things that we're doing that none of this matters.

With that level of personal connection it might seem strange that Dan and I both decided fairly early on that we wanted someone else to run the company and we brought in an external CEO. I'm Creative Director now, and the business has grown beyond the initial idea; Dan and I just weren't the right people to develop the business model. I guess I have stepped aside in a way, but that's because above everything I'm determined that this must work, and it really must work beyond me. I'm completely committed to that more than I'm committed to my ego.

My top tips

"Two heads are better than one. If you can find the right person to develop an idea with, it's a beautiful experience with lots of brainstorming to reach the right idea. It also takes lots of blood, sweat and tears to make an idea come to fruition, and having a partner to share that with is a real help."

"I think the worst mistake in the world can be (but not always) when the people who have the idea end up running the business. Don't worry about letting go because a good idea, if you're still influencing it, will translate into a good business if you have the right people there."

"If you get VC funding make sure that you've got enough to really start out proper. At the beginning we only achieved half of what we were looking for, and as a consequence of that we've had to go through a whole round of different funding which has used up precious time and energy that should have gone into the business."

My call to arms

"I'd like three major companies in three different sectors to go CarbonNeutral in a big way in the next year, and for them to communicate that in a big way. I'd like an oil company, an automotive company, and a mobile communications company because I think those are going to have the biggest reach on consumers."

"I'd like the government to provide support for those companies who go CarbonNeutral. Years ago there was a government scheme where companies who supported the arts could apply for cash to help them communicate what they were doing. If this happened for CarbonNeutral I think it would really encourage a ripple effect."

Ideas you can steal

Don't preach to the converted

Sue was clearly not keen to hire people from the voluntary sector. Although to some this might sound slightly controversial, it's generally true that salesmen, not activists, make sales. If your idea is credible, there's no reason why you need to recruit people whose only qualification is a passion for the issue; find the people that know how sales work, know spreadsheets, know distribution. OK you don't want a heartless capitalist, but you do need proven ability.

Make it 'edible'

Climate change has long been a great intangible issue, but Sue spent years crafting a solution that people could, and therefore would, buy into. Many other social and environmental issues are complex, projects struggle to connect people to their particular causes and solutions. We think the principles behind the CarbonNeutral equation can provide stimulus for other projects to find their hook to the public; use its principles as a benchmark and you'll come up with some great solutions for your venture.

Emotional sells need creative expression

Many solutions to social or environmental issues will deliver a benefit to those whom you manage to engage, but it's often not the kind of immediate or 'hard' benefit that (especially business) people are accustomed to. Therefore these issues don't always sit well within conventional presentations, as Sue found in Newcastle. If it's an emotional sell, use images, use video, use people; the issues might have previously seemed intangible and unrelated to the audience, so you'll need to work hard to connect them.

An idea isn't an idea until you can sell it

Sue was very clear on this; pieces of paper with thoughts on social change don't constitute an idea. An idea is only worth something when you've put the time in to grow it to be something that can be executed, sold, enacted; don't rest until you know exactly how your idea will look and work 'on the shelf'.

Get friends on the inside

Most social or environmental issues have the capacity to pull on a heart string, and this means you have two advantages over commercial initiatives that are taken to corporates: you can engage corporate people on a personal level, and some of those people will become champions of your venture within their company. Sue has had great success in unearthing 'evangelists' within companies to help make CarbonNeutral happen 'from the inside'.

Trevor Baylis

The wind-up radio: a radio that uses a winding mechanism to generate its own power, allowing information to be communicated to poor and remote areas not served by electricity.

Why he's here...

Trevor resembles the classic English 'garden shed' inventor, right down to his pipe smoking and the tools and prototypes that litter his workshop. But Trevor is no mere tinkerer; we've chosen him because he has a rare ability to become immersed in a problem, think in 3-D, and express himself through physical solutions. Trevor's 'way' is a lesson in how to be creative. Add to that the fact that his wind-up radio is one of the iconic social inventions of the last century that addresses one of the most challenging issues facing the developing world, and you have a pretty special story.

Who is Trevor Baylis?

Trevor was born in 1937 in Kilburn, north-west London and brought up in Southall, west London. He left school at 15 and whilst not academically minded, he was a highly accomplished swimmer and represented Great Britain in an international competition that same year.

His first job was in a soil mechanics lab, which enabled him to study mechanical and structural engineering. After completing his national service as a physical training instructor he became a swimming pool salesman. That led him to become a professional swimmer, then an aquatic stunt man, then an underwater escapologist in a Berlin circus.

In 1985 Trevor designed a range of products for disabled people called Orange Aids, and followed that up in 1991 with the wind-up radio.

In 1997 he was awarded an OBE for humanitarian services to Africa. He's also met with Nelson Mandela, completed international lecture tours with the British Council, been honoured with numerous academic and civil awards, and been the subject of several television programmes including This is Your Life.

The issues he confronted

There are currently estimated to be nearly 40 million people living with HIV/AIDS globally. In the last year the AIDS epidemic claimed more than 3 million lives, and close to 5 million people became infected with HIV. Around 95% of people suffering through HIV/AIDS live in developing nations.

The UNAIDS programme identifies that 'Information, education and communication are among the most important elements of the response to AIDS: only with awareness and accurate knowledge of HIV is it possible to take effective action'.

1.6 billion people don't have access to electricity, making the transfer of information and public health messages in the developing world very difficult.

The solution he created

The wind-up radio ensures that fundamentally life-saving health related messages can be easily communicated to poor and remote communities in the developing world.

There are now several versions of the radio, including solar powered models. It is distributed through charitable and NGO channels, as well as through sales.

The radio is also an iconic product for camping enthusiasts and design buffs alike.

Trevor's story

What I'm all about

When I was a boy I couldn't write my name, but I could do the most amazing essays in steel. In other words I found it easier to express myself using my hands. I could speak, I just didn't much like writing. A picture's worth a thousand words, a prototype's worth a million words, and a dream is worth a billion words because you can do what you like in your mind. For me that's what all this is about. The fun part of the exercise is making it tangible. I'm lucky, I'm surrounded by machinery and tools and contraptions which I've gathered over the years in my work room, and I spend my time pratting around. That's what it's all about.

I don't want to be the richest man in the graveyard; you can only eat one meal at a time, you can only wear one suit at a time, and I hate wearing suits. The thought of getting up at half past six every morning, putting on a suit, and making my way to the East End of London just to climb up in a bloody tower looking out over some bloody gas works… no thanks.

Swim, cane, educate

I was born during the war when every night was fireworks night, and I didn't get much of an education because we never knew whether the school would still be standing the next day. I failed my eleven-plus so I was a B-streamer throughout secondary school, and instead of studying I used to sneak off with my mate to go swimming in the canal at Southall which is full of dead dogs and God knows what. When my parents found out they went ape and packed me off to Southall swimming pool. My cousin Derek taught me how to swim, then I joined Heston swimming club, and there I really did learn to swim. So every morning I used to get up at half past five, get on my bike and cycle to Heston. We'd swim for a couple of hours and then I'd cycle back to school. Of course I was invariably late, and so I'd get a caning, and then I'd be educated. So it was swim, cane, educate, swim, cane, educate, and this went on for many years. But I got good at swimming and I competed for Middlesex, then the Southern Counties, and then Great Britain. And then things changed; the headmaster suddenly said "Oh Trevor, why didn't you tell me?" and of course he was very agreeable from then on and I could turn up at quarter past nine if I wanted to. Swimming played a big important part in my life; it was my first love and it really gave me confidence in myself for the first time.

It's all Polish to me

When I left school I was thinking about going into the police force but I was too short; you had to be 5' 8" and I was about 5' 6" with my umbrella up. Instead

I got a job in soil mechanics, and this meant I had to study mechanical and structural engineering, and all of a sudden I discovered that I could use my brain and, in fact, I thoroughly enjoyed it. My old exercise books talk about 'ordinary differential equations'; it's written in my fair hand but now I can't even read them; it could be in Polish. So, when I was exposed to the right stuff I was a bright guy.

From salesman to stunt man

When I finished national service I wanted to find a job that combined swimming with engineering, so I joined one of the companies that made the first of the free-standing swimming pools; Purley Pools they were called. We used to do the Ideal Home exhibition, and I would stand in front of a pool wearing my electric blue suit; 'Hello John, you want to buy a swimming pool?' We weren't getting any sales so I said to my governor 'Any chance of a swim?' I plunged in the pool, started swimming up and down, and the next thing we know there's this enormous crowd around the pool. 'Hang on, hang on, we're selling pools here' said my governor, and that's when I became a professional display swimmer.

A little while later I was doing my tumbling and tricks and God knows what at the Boat Show, a fellow came up to me and asked if I'd ever thought of doing any stunt work. One thing led to another and I found myself driving cars into rivers, doing fire dives off high towers, falling off bridges, falling off the decks of boats. I also did an underwater escape act in a Berlin circus where they blindfolded me, roped me up, put me into a sarcophagus, nailed the lid on it and dropped me into 10 feet of water, and the idea was to get myself out and take a compliment.

Amputee for an hour

So, that's my background; then I started making these things called Orange Aids which were pieces of kit to help the disabled. Why? Because I have always believed that stunt players and disabled people are kinfolk. I saw a number of my stunt player friends breaking themselves up; on the last trick they did they hit the wall. In that game disability is only a banana skin away, and the tragedy is that when you see somebody in a chair you just presume they've always been disabled. You can never visualise them as a stunt player or anything else; you don't realise that many of these people had a life before they were disabled.

I thought to myself one day: 'I wonder what it's like to be disabled'. So, I took my right hand, which is my dominant hand, put it in my pocket, and my girlfriend at the time, strapped my arm to my side and I didn't take my hand out of my pocket for one hour. I spent that hour walking around the house to see what it was like just to have one arm. It was impossible to do things. How do you take a top off a bottle with one hand? You try and stuff it between your knees, you try jamming it in the door, you try anything to hold on to it. I realised just how much you rely on having both hands available, so I developed a whole range of products that replaced what one hand would be doing, based around solving the simple, practical problems like opening a bottle. It's like a grown-up version of Meccano with a series of vices and straps and levers, which all fit onto a simple permanent casting on a wheel chair or a table, and it allows disabled people to get by. I had them coated with thick orange paint, and I called them Orange Aids.

I was very proud of Orange Aids and I had big plans that we would have a factory staffed by disabled people, but the company who was bought in to help basically worked me out of the programme. That was a lesson I tell you.

An African vision

A little while later, in about 1991, I was sitting in my living room watching TV and there was a program on about HIV/AIDS in Africa. The message of the show was that the only way they could stop this thing was with education, which would best be brought to the 600 million people across Africa using radio. But there was one major problem; most of Africa doesn't have electricity. The only portable form of electricity came in batteries, but they were horrendously expensive and you'd have people bartering their maize and their rice to get hold of them.

So I start to think about the problem, and suddenly I'm in this dream state. I'm imagining myself in a white pith helmet sitting somewhere in Africa, I've got my pipe in my mouth, a gin and tonic in my hand, and I'm listening to some raunchy number by Dame Nellie Melba on my wind-up gramophone with a horn on top. 'Hang on, if you can get all this noise by dragging a rusty nail around a piece of old bakelight using a spring, surely there's enough power in the spring to drive a dynamo, which in turn would drive a radio?' And that is how the wind-up radio came about, through a silly dream.

I headed out to my shed and started playing around. The first thing I did was to check that a radio would play like this, so I attached a small dynamo into a hand drill, joined two wires to a cheap radio, turned the handle, and I got the first bite of sound. Then I went out into the garden and got a bucket of water, put a string on it and ran it up next door's tree, put it over a pulley and I brought it down to a handle. As the bucket slowly descended it turned the handle, which through a compound gearbox drove a dynamo which was attached to a radio, and the radio played. So that was the first wind-up radio. My neighbour popped his head over the

fence and asked how long it would play for; I told him it depended how tall the tree was.

'You must be mad; it'll never work'

I then started playing around with different sizes and types of springs and before long we had a proper prototype. I got myself a patent attorney, Jacqueline Needelin was her name, she filed for a patent for me and then I started hawking it around. Everybody turned me down! 'You must be daft', 'You must be crazy', 'It wouldn't work unless the spring weighed a hundred weight'. I've got classic rejection letters from all the big players, including one from the Design Council saying how it would never work and nobody could afford it and all that crap; that letter's now framed on my wall.

I nearly gave up at that point but then the BBC went wild for it. It was given to the Tomorrow's World team and suddenly from getting rejections left, right and centre we had a TV show. The Tomorrow's World team did a fantastic job and all of a sudden I was getting phone calls. One of these calls was from a fellow called Christopher Stones who worked for BDO Stoy Hayward, a firm of accountants. We sat down together, and soon enough we were in production.

Poetry

The really great thing came when Christopher brought in this large insurance company called Liberty Life who helped us set up a factory in Cape Town staffed by disabled people. I'd pushed that from day one, and because of my work with Orange Aids I was really chuffed to have made it happen. In Africa the poor who are disabled don't get the facilities that you and I would anticipate; not so much as a walking stick. When it all happened like that I thought the thing was poetry.

Me being a bit of a showman the media really picked up on things and I found myself doing all sorts of interesting stuff like the Big Breakfast show. All of a sudden my personality came back out and it was just like my stunt days; it became show time again. In my bedroom I've got 11 of what I call my ego files, most people call

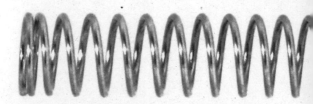

them scrap books, where I've kept all the press cuttings about me and the radio. That's 11 albums, three inches thick. Now if you think how much it would cost to get that sort of publicity; we're talking about millions and millions of pounds.

In the middle of all this the BBC decided to take me off to Africa to film an episode of QED. They'd prearranged everything and didn't actually tell me what was going to happen. We went into Cape Town and visited the factory, and then we headed off to this house in Pretoria, and blow me if it wasn't Nelson Mandela's house. We turned up and suddenly there's Nelson Mandela, and he was charming. He took us in, looked after us, gave us a few cups of tea, and he really liked what we were doing. That bloke's a saint; what a remarkable man.

Radios in the field

A little while later I returned to Africa and I remember going to a little village somewhere in Botswana, and there must have been about 300 people gathered around my radio all doing rock and roll dancing. We take our facilities so much for granted in England. Our biggest technology issue is the size of our TV screen. Poverty in Africa is on a scale that we just can't begin to image.

I've left the original company in Cape Town because they moved their operations to China and let's just say I disagreed with that decision. There are now several companies making wind-up radios, and everybody is competing to provide the best quality at the lowest cost, which I guess has to be a good thing.

The next thing in wind-up

I've got a few things going on at the moment. When I was in Botswana I attended the Commonwealth Conference and in front of a thousand people I connected one of my radios to an Apple iMac computer with a couple of wires. We wound the thing up as far as it could go and, briefly, for about 30 seconds, a screen came up. What I basically proved was that in the future we may well have wind-up computers and that's something I'm working on with my friends at Bristol University.

I've also invented a pair of shoes which generate electricity as you walk; they're actually in the Guinness Book of Records. I once wore them to walk across the Namibian desert and when I got to the other side I phoned Richard Branson on my mobile which had been charged by the shoes. Funnily enough he was one of the guys who initially turned me down on the radio, but that's alright, he's a nice enough chap. Unfortunately if you wore the shoes nowadays, you'd look like a shoe bomber, so I discontinued it.

Most of my energies though are spent trying to help other inventors and I do that through something called Baylis Brands. We basically run a service where independent inventors can bring us their ideas and we'll check them over for them. I'm also vice-president of the European Women of Achievement awards, because I'm very keen to help bring women inventors to the fore. If you think about it, how many people can name three women scientists, three women engineers, or three women inventors. The vast majority of people can't. The education system's up the shoot when there are more women on this earth than there are blokes and we can't answer those simple questions. There's an amazing amount of talent out there and we should be using it, otherwise as a race we're just underachieving.

My top tips

"If you've got a good idea, don't go and tell everybody about it because somebody will steal it from you."

"When you can see an answer to an issue, get off your backside and do something about it."

"If you think you've got something tangible then please contact Baylis Brands. Read the website first to make sure you're happy with what we offer, and then get in touch and we'll see if we can help."

My call to arms

"The UK has got to recognise those ordinary men and women who have the most extraordinary ability to change all our lives both socially and commercially. When it comes to creating inventors this country is still supreme, but we are absolutely appalling at bringing their inventions to the marketplace. The government needs to recognise this and support organisations such as mine that will protect inventors and prevent their ideas from being taken from them. This is the only way we'll get the most back from our citizens."

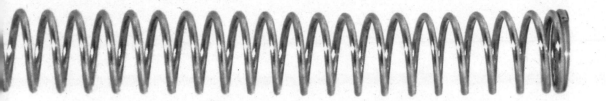

Ideas you can steal

Live the issue you're confronting

When Trevor decided to create something to help disabled people he lived the life of an amputee for an hour, and that gave him the insight to be able to create workable solutions. Too many solutions to social issues are imposed from the outside with no real understanding of what it's like to suffer the actual issue. Always try and live the problem you want to confront when you're designing your intervention.

Think differently about how you attract support

Trevor was rejected by every conventional channel of support for his invention, and his breakthrough really came in reverse; a TV show was made about the radio and then the money men came in. Sometimes you need to turn the model on its head, especially when you're seeking support from those bodies that are so inundated with requests they might not spot the true worth of your enterprise.

Think how other people might approach the issue

When he was thinking about how to get the message to people with no electricity, Trevor dreamt up how a similar problem was approached from another perspective; how did the colonial gents get their gramophone to work in that same environment? He basically stole a principle from another solution that was addressing the same issue. Take time to think about how other people, other places, other sectors deal with the principles of your issue and you will generate new ideas.

Bring down the global issues

The wind-up radio is a great example of a small solution that takes on a big issue. But, when developing solutions like this one it's unlikely that you could make the leap directly from the big issue (combating HIV/AIDS) to an achievable solution (wind-up technology); you have to break the overarching issue down into manageable problems that you can tackle. In this case the breakdown goes: the spread of HIV/AIDS, to lack of education, to lack of electricity; the problem gets simplified and then the solution pops out; wind-up technology. If you are facing a seemingly insurmountable challenge, break it down to the underlying problems and you'll find it much easier to generate ideas.

Carmel McConnell

Magic Breakfast: provides nutritious breakfasts in UK primary schools to combat the problem of young kids arriving at school too hungry to learn.

Why she's here...

We chose Carmel because she embodies that meeting of head and heart that we think makes a great social entrepreneur. She started out as a front-line protester and then rose through the ranks of one of the UK's biggest corporate companies. Now she brings the best of those two worlds together to challenge one of the UK's most pressing social issues. You can really see this in the way that she's funded her organisation; a commercial arm supporting the social mission - a model that we think is the most effective way forward for social enterprise. Add to all this Carmel's boundless energy and sheer dedication to hungry school kids and you've got a formidable social entrepreneur.

?WHAT IF! UnLtd*

Who is Carmel?

Carmel left school at 15 and held various jobs before going to university. There, she became involved in protesting against Cruise missiles entering the Greenham Common airbase near Newbury, Berkshire. She was arrested and imprisoned as a 'civil objector'. This event awakened Carmel's social conscience and helped set her on the road to social activism.

In the early nineties she carried out a campaigning speaking tour across the United States and became involved with the Native American rights movement through the Jesse Jackson Rainbow Coalition. She then got stuck into grassroots activism in the UK, including anti-deportation campaigns.

Carmel worked for BT for several years in many different roles before leaving to set up a consultancy, Holistic Management, to advise big business on corporate social responsibility. Her clients include Twentieth Century Fox, BT and Hewlett Packard.

In 2001, Carmel wrote her first book, Change Activist, and started delivering breakfasts to schools in Hackney, East London. A year later, she launched Magic Outcomes, a professional training company which offers companies a unique, schools-based development programme and which donates all profits to the Magic Breakfast.

The issues she confronted

Hunger at school, apathy, and lack of nutritional education creates a self-perpetuating spiral of disadvantage: children at school who are hungry or don't eat nutritious food are less able to concentrate, and so don't learn effectively; they consequently risk having lower paid jobs as adults. This cycle of poverty continues through generations.

Relative poverty – defined as families with an income of less than half the national average – is widespread in the UK: in 2003/2004 28% or 3.5 million children, were classified as poor, compared to 1.4 million in 1979.

Children in deprived wards often arrive at school too hungry to learn; in many cases, the school meal will be the only hot meal they receive during the day. A survey by the Doctor Patient Partnership in May 2001 showed that one quarter of UK children eat sweets and crisps for breakfast.

The solution she created

The Magic Breakfast aims to break this cycle for potentially millions of children by providing 'fuel for learning': nutritious breakfasts that give children the energy they need to concentrate in class. The project works in close partnership with schools, parents, business and the government to provide nutrition education and awareness raising events for the whole school community.

The sister operation, the training organisation Magic Outcomes, invests 100% of its profits in Magic Breakfast. Funds raised from sales of Carmel's best-selling business title, Change Activist, are also donated.

In 2002 the Magic Breakfast delivered 3,600 breakfasts; this number had risen to around 70,000 by 2004.

Carmel's story

From political action to magical outcomes

The Greenham Common protests were the turning point for me. I'd never been in trouble, never stepped out of line and certainly never been arrested. When I left school at 15, all I was really focused on, like any other teenager was earning some money and having fun. Having a social conscience didn't really come into it. The only insight I had was from my father, who taught me about Irish history and how it fitted into the rest of the world. In particular he showed me how the Irish were similar to his friends who were immigrants from India and Jamaica (he worked in the Foundry at Ford, Dagenham), in that the only reason we were all in England was because we needed to earn a living. So I was lucky to grow up with samosas and patties as much as bacon and cabbage.

After five years' working, I got to university, and in my first term I went to a peace protest to write something for the student uni magazine. While there, someone asked if I could stay and help by sitting in the road to help block the builders getting into the military base at Greenham Common. I said no, thought about it for five minutes, and then changed my mind. The idea was to stop the base being built for Cruise missiles. Basically the US military had decided to put missiles (for aggressive or "first strike" use) just outside Newbury in Berkshire. There was a group of Welsh mothers who were passionate about stopping the missiles and they helped me realise how important it was for ordinary people like me to stand up (or in this case sit down) and be counted.

That protest event was a big wake up call for me. I ended up living in at the camp for several years, being imprisoned a few times, being arrested many, many times. Most importantly, I had a crash course in peaceful social activism, learned more about social history, especially how Gandhi and the suffragettes had made change happen against the odds. I became convinced that our little protest could stop the US military. And, after several years, it did.

Questioning everything

What I learned during that time changed my life. I realised that the news on TV or in the papers wasn't always true. I learned in particular, from being arrested and put in prison, to make connections with lots of other things. It was a shock being on a remand wing, talking to women who hadn't done anything worse than be too poor to pay the bills. The need to campaign for an end to US nukes in the UK led me to do things like walk into the House of Commons with a pram full of chains and banners; at one point I tried to lasso myself to Margaret Thatcher which you wouldn't really want to do unless you were desperate to make a point!

So I became an activist for change. As time went on, I was fortunate enough to be able to use the same ideas to improve how big companies work: that the principles of social improvement can be applied to making money. For example, consumer trust means consumer loyalty – so I was interested in how to make that happen, and how to treat staff with respect and honesty. That was, and is, controversial, but I am a firm believer that being able to create wealth and to use it wisely, is a critical skill for social activists. Much later in my career I had the chance to put my 'activist-turned-corporate-campaigner' story into a business title, called Change Activist. It was while I was researching Change Activist that I discovered the staggering statistic that for one in four kids in the UK, the only hot food they get is at school. Also that, most shockingly, despite the UK being the fourth richest country in the world, we rate 23rd out of 29 European countries for child malnutrition.

Putting on a business hat

So I started thinking OK, while I'm still running my consultancy why not just drop some breakfast food off at a few schools and see if that makes a difference? I spent about a year buying food from the local supermarket in Hackney and dropping it round at schools on Saturday mornings in my car. The feedback from teachers was so positive that I decided to reduce my business consultancy and expand deliveries, thereby starting the Magic Breakfast.

What I didn't want was to have rely on grant funding, I was adamant that it should become self-financing; I knew that was the only way that we could make it truly effective and sustainable over the long term. I realised that there was a big market for business to get involved and to learn first hand about social responsibility, while at the same time taking back something that would really benefit them; for example, developing leadership and teambuilding skills.

So, in 2002 I started Magic Outcomes, the Magic Breakfast's sister organisation. This is the real social enterprise part, now providing most of the funding for Magic Breakfast. It's an innovative business which provides schools-based training and development programmes to organisations which want to pursue their commercial objectives hand in hand with socially responsible outcomes. So far, Pearson, Unilever and BT have sent employees on leadership or team-building programmes, and our fees, after costs, go to the food deliveries. For every person who does one of our leadership programmes, we can give breakfasts to two schools.

Thinking big, staying focused

I never set out to be a 'career' social entrepreneur. Once I saw that statistic about how many kids were going hungry, I simply wanted to find a way to solve the problem. Right now some young children arrive at school too hungry to learn. That is simply shocking in the UK, the fourth richest economy in the world. So what is the most direct way to solve that? Answer: deliver food to the schools in most need, then work out how to help schools solve the problem long term. So, taking action is the first thing even if the plan isn't watertight or the answer isn't 100% right, do something and then learn as you go. The most important thing to ask with any new opportunity is 'does this serve our purpose or is it a distraction?' If a new activity doesn't result in more healthy food for primary schools in need, we don't do it. Well, we try not to!

Remembering what counts

My home life always comes first. Maybe that's sacrilege to say, but I've been through various stages of my life being an activist and doing nothing but being an activist, forgetting family and friends, and I don't think that's very healthy. My partner Catherine and my younger sister Caroline, are the most important things in my whole life. Without them I wouldn't be doing anything. My relationship and my family come first, really and truly, and then I build from there. To be a long-term social entrepreneur I feel it's a good idea to remember your own home life and happiness, as well as solving the social issue. So if my sister or partner needs me to do something, that will come before a Magic Breakfast request. Simple as that.

I also think it's very important to work out what you are good at, and what makes you happy and focus on those. Don't go against the flow of who you really are. It wouldn't work if I was the numbers person; my role is to be out there persuading, linking partners, making the vision a reality. What I really enjoy is being a social broker, connecting people, ideas and resources, because fantastic solutions often come from chance conversations. For example, we have my publisher Pearson to thank for our office space in London – and they only knew we needed somewhere for our work through a chance comment. So I think it's important to encourage networks, ask people for their views and be open to new ways of thinking. Much better than trying to work it all out yourself!

My Irish background also means I love feeding people, so of course I'm happy to be providing a breakfast which means that a previously hungry kid is full enough to concentrate and get the most from his lessons. I really feel honoured to have the chance to do this.

Embracing the 'N' word

I had a call this morning from a woman who wants us to help her work out ideas for a new food product to sell to the youth market. I had to say no. We get so many interesting calls, but we simply haven't got enough resources to be able to give the advice we would like to, to help everyone. The priority is to offer a really good resource to schools, and to raise the funds to continue expanding school food delivery.

We're also going to continue our lobbying work alongside the food deliveries and Magic Outcomes. This year it looks like we'll be delivering about 90-100,000 breakfasts, up 20,000 from last year. That's a phenomenal amount, but it's just the tip of the iceberg. We'll have to evolve in whatever way that solves the problem. If we were to continue like this, in two years' time we'd be delivering a million breakfasts every single year. Do I want to be running a huge logistical organisation? God forbid. That's never been my game plan. So we need to be focusing on more lobbying, and at working with more schools to see how we can squeeze every last penny into getting decent food for the kids. We need to make the case for an end to child hunger through improved government policy as well as through delivering food to schools.

The best of both worlds

In my opinion, the best way forward is to get the best out of both the private and the public sector. What does that mean? Be the most passionate, caring social activist and create sustainable, social improvement. And do this while being entrepreneurial and building your organisational capacity.

I suppose that for me, having a social activist background combined with commercial experience meant that social enterprise was a natural step. Just as I believe social enterprise is the next evolutionary stage for mainstream profit-making firms. I believe that social entrepreneurs have a role in evolving the business world as well, so that what I call profit and principle are seen as an equal goal.

Staying true to yourself

I think that you can only hope to make a difference in the world if you are honest with yourself and know who you are and what matters to you. The way I see it, you have two choices: to do something that will challenge and engage you and will feed your soul, or to create a life based around distraction and status and toys. So many people plan to live their lives later, when the kids are grown, when they've saved enough money. I say to people, live your life now, not later. We don't get forever to do this. Also, be optimistic. Ask yourself, what small thing could you do that would make a difference? If you start today, by thinking about the kind of world you'd like to live in, I bet some kind of action follows naturally. Magic Breakfast started with baby steps, and so can anything.

Ideas you can steal

Play for both teams

Carmel has the ideal background to be a social entrepreneur because she has worked on 'both sides'; she's been a campaigner and she's worked in a corporate environment. Now she combines her knowledge and expertise of those two worlds to deliver Magic Breakfast. Social entrepreneurship needs those two components for it to exist, and it's great that Carmel brings them in one person. We know not everyone has that combination of experience and we're not suggesting you suddenly need to take on a business degree or volunteer in Africa for a year, but do partner with someone who will help you bring together the best of both worlds.

Earn your own crust

Because Carmel has used Magic Outcomes to create her own funding mechanism, Magic Breakfast is not subject to the traumas that often come with public sector funding. Being in control of your own income is a real advantage for a social enterprise; it stops you constantly looking for your next round of investment, having to meet the varying criteria of different funding bodies, or suffering as a result of a shift in government agenda or public opinion which might mean your cash goes elsewhere. We also think that earned income brings with it a certain set of commercial and entrepreneurial dynamics that are very positive for a venture. If there is a way to avoid the mysteries, frustrations and complexities of charitable and government funding, we would definitely suggest you follow Carmel's example.

Passion and anger!

The beginnings of Magic Breakfast were wonderfully simple; Carmel read that some kids were going to school too hungry to learn so she went and bought them breakfast. The rest, as they say, is history. We think this shows the level of passion or anger you need about the issue you're confronting, and the proactive instinct you need to go beyond just writing proposals to actually make change happen. (It's 'moments' like this that also make for great stories when you need to articulate your project and inspire others to support you).

Siobhan Freegard

netmums: a series of locally based websites for mums (and dads) aimed at helping people cope with and enjoy parenthood. It offers listings of local services, provides a forum for people to ask each other questions, and it allows people to make new parenting friends.

Why she's here...

Siobhan has created a solution to a major parenting issue and netmums has grown so rapidly that we think it has the potential to become an institution for British parents. The model is one that can almost self replicate wherever there is a mum with the passion to create a netmums site in her community; that is the sort of replication model that would be prized by any entrepreneur, social or otherwise. We can only guess at the impact netmums will have long-term, but when you allow parents to feel good you get happier kids, happier communities, and we think, a better future for society generally.

?WHAT IF! UnLtd*

Who is Siobhan?

- Siobhan's from a small town just outside Dublin. She left for the bright lights of London at 18 where she started out on her career.

- She worked her way up the corporate ladder in various sales and marketing roles, including Marketing Director for one of the Wembley Group companies.

- Siobhan started netmums after she had her first son and experienced feeling isolated as a mother. She now has three children and runs netmums full-time.

The issues she confronted

- Because of recent demographic and social changes, modern-day mothers often lack traditional support structures: families and friends live apart from each other and communities aren't as tight-knit as they used to be.

- In a recent survey of 2,000 mothers, 60% didn't have the help of extended family, 60% didn't have friends to replace their family, and 50% had suffered from post-natal depression.

The solution she created

- netmums is an online community for new parents, which provides a range of information, networking and friendship building opportunities. Local parents host their own regional sites and members feed in and share information.

- netmums now has 164 local sites listed throughout the UK, and 120,000 members. The website is free to users and is funded through advertising by companies relevant to parents. It's a limited company, but describes itself as a social enterprise.

Siobhan's story

To be or not to be a full-time mum

Although I didn't go to university and I hated school I've always been very career-oriented. For a long time I worked hard and played hard, and my husband and I thrived on the 'double-income-no-kids-yet' type of lifestyle. My life had always been centred around work and that was the environment where I guess I felt safe; even when I was pregnant with our first child I think I was kind of in denial so I pretty much worked right up until the baby arrived.

This all meant that I was completely unprepared for the emotional side of having a child, unprepared for the bond that comes with it and I struggled with a feeling of being out of control. Suddenly I had this new need to be at home and to be a full-time mother. It conflicted with everything I knew of myself and I spent about two years struggling to re-establish a sense of normality when I would go back to work, then decide to stay home, then go back to work...

When my husband and I finally decided that I'd stay at home, everyone thought 'no way, she'll be bored within six months', but I was determined to make a go of it. I remember clearly when that first Monday morning came and my husband went off to work; suddenly there I was tidying up, playing with Lego, waiting on the baby. I went into this kind of overdrive where In the space of 45 minutes I'd done everything a full-time mum plans to do in a day, but there was still this long day stretching ahead of me before my husband was due home. It's funny because it sounds great having a whole day to yourself but the reality is you can't just lie around watching TV, and all it did for me was generate this horrible sense of isolation. My husband once called at six to say he was going to be home an hour late and I just broke down in tears on the phone because I had to face this extra hour being alone.

I was a modern phenomenon

Looking back and having been involved with netmums I know now that I was just a one of the 60% of women who go through that experience and feel exactly the same way. It's just what happens in today's society; people no longer settle down with people in the same road as their parents or their cousins, we all move away, we meet husbands and partners that come from different parts of the world, we have children later so we are not having them at the same time as our friends... This all means that society is far more fragmented, and that was me.

Getting out there

Then one day I heard about this mother and toddler group that was held in the church hall every Wednesday. So I took myself off to this hall and there were about 15 mums there with kids the same age as mine, and I thought, wow this is great; suddenly there were all these other women that would really 'get' what I was going through, and maybe I could start making friends. I didn't get off to a great start, and in the first few sessions I was a bit like the new kid in the playground, but I remember one day I spotted a mum who had this great pair of trainers on, and I love fashion so I went over and started a conversation. From that point on life just got better; I made friends and I began to feel settled. I even went on to become the kind of Grande Dame of the group because I would always spot the new mum walking into the room with that look in their eyes that I'd had, that unsure, helpless look, and I'd make a point of going up and saying hello and introducing them to everyone.

Becoming a resource

I soon started to find other things that I could do on various days of the week; there was swimming on a Monday, the mother and baby cinema session on a Tuesday... When someone then asked me what else there was for mums in the area I decided to write it down for them, and before I knew it I was making photocopies and handouts and becoming a walking resource centre! That's fundamentally where the idea of netmums started from: I wanted to help other mothers avoid those really tough times early on and not to experience what I went through. No-one will ever come and knock on your door and say 'Oh, you're a new mum, how can I help you?' So I wanted to create something a bit like a guide book which says, 'this is what it's like, and here's what you can do'.

The obvious home for this guide book was the internet which was really taking off at time, but it was hard to get people engaged to support me in those early days. I'd explain the idea of a web-based resource for mums and people would just nod encouragingly but not really take it seriously. When I did get other mums to offer up some of their ideas, I didn't personally have the organisational skills to get everything together in a way that would work. Luckily, Sally Russell, a friend of mine who's a brilliant organiser sat down with me and we pooled our resources and hammered out a basic structure for a website, just for the Harrow area. 'Women on the Web' was my first choice of name, but as a testament to just how naïve I was about the internet that turned out to be a porn site, so I went with netmums instead.

A virtual cooperative

When we launched we didn't really have very high expectations, but before we knew it we had 100 members signed up. We'd only told a few people, so how on earth they heard about us so quickly I'll never know. And not only were we growing fast, all

these people were giving us feedback, saying 'you've missed out a toddler group', 'you've missed a city farm'… so the resource really grew through people sharing, like a kind of virtual cooperative.

The next big development was when those members began asking questions: 'I'm going through a hard time at the moment, is that normal?', or 'My child's not eating, what should I do?' So, we began to develop a question and answer forum where people could go to each other for advice. This soon led to what I think is the most successful part of the site, the 'Meet a Mum' section, where you exchange emails with people in your area, and hopefully make new friends.

Going nationwide!

We'd never really planned to take netmums beyond Harrow, until one day when we got an email from a woman in Leicestershire, asking if we ran anything similar in her area. We said 'No, but here's the template and the software, you fill in the gaps'. That got us thinking: mums are mums, and whether they're in Harrow or Harrogate they all go through the same experiences. So we set about replicating the idea. We took three areas: Kensington and Chelsea where you have very rich and very poor living side by side; Hillingdon, which like Harrow is quite suburban; and Leicestershire, which covers rural areas. The results in each were exactly the same as our experience in Harrow: in each area we got 100 members just by word of mouth, plus we started to get requests from mums all over the country saying 'Can we have one here?'

When we got to six sites we began having to dig into our own pockets, and that actually means my husband's credit card which made him none too pleased. It was just getting too big for us to do by ourselves, we needed cash and we needed to be able to employ people to do the inputting. So I wrote to the marketing director at Tesco and that was our first big break. They loved the idea and made us an offer: they wanted us to build 40 new sites in 40 different areas over the course of a year, and here's £120k to do it. That was an amazing moment; Tesco just 'got it'. The concept fitted exactly with what they wanted to get across, that communities matter. They believed like us that mums are effectively the centre of the community: when you bring mums together, you bring families together, you get happy mums which

means happy kids, happy dads, happy communities. We were the perfect fit for their overall marketing drive.

A hiccup

By the end of the year we had something like 5,000 members and were over the moon with our progress, but we ran into a problem. We were hoping for a three year deal with Tesco, but because they were already committed to another initiative we lost out. That was really gutting; we'd built up this fantastic thing and it seemed it was all going to be knocked down again. So we went on a desperate search for another investor and eventually found four companies willing to sponsor us: Huggies, Nick Jr, Early Learning Centre and BT. Again, it made good business sense for them: Huggies uses our website to tell our members (their core consumer) about events or clubs, and they can use our site to test their products in a very honest forum.

Not ticking the right box

At the moment we're lobbying to get government funding to help us take another step up, but it's proving difficult because we don't fit their fairly narrow view of the world. In their eyes we're not reaching the most in-need mothers because we're not specifically targeting areas of poverty; this opinion totally misses the point. Often it's the girls in the council houses who actually have better support because they haven't moved away from the area in which they grew up and their family and friends remain near by. That sounds horribly patronising, and obviously I'm not saying that's true of everywhere, but often whatever the other issues on an estate there will be a healthy support network. It's the middle-class mums who come out of the workplace, don't have babies until their mid-thirties, and although they may live in a slightly nicer house, they can be much more isolated. There are no kids playing in the street, no communal bench where people sit and chat, no family a few doors down. It's these mums who the government need to realise are more likely to feel isolated and become depressed, and should therefore be classed as being disadvantaged.

One bit of hope in terms of government is that Sally, my colleague, is on an Office of the Deputy Prime Minister committee and is working with the government to launch a helpline for parents. At least here we're having the opportunity to have an input based on what our members are saying is important to them.

Growing up

We now have 120,000 members and we're hoping that's going to grow over the next two years to 1 million. It sounds like a lot but it's a really realistic target if you think that there are 6.5 million parents of kids under the age of 16 in the UK, and of course the more people that join the more dynamic it becomes. We're heading in the right direction; at the moment when a person puts a request on our Meet a Mum page we get 20 responses, and we recently calculated that a thousand new friendships have been made in 2005 alone through the meeting boards.

Everyone says that parenting is one of the hardest jobs in the world and that's so true, but you don't get a manual or have lessons at school and it's hard to know where to go for help these days. My big wish is that netmums will one day be part of the fabric of society, so that when you first find out you're pregnant and have that excited feeling, the next thing you do is sign up to netmums. Then when the big day comes you'll already have the networks and the support that everyone needs to enjoy being a parent.

My top tips

"Mothers should speak to each other more and look out for one another. Go to the mother and toddler groups and when you do spot someone with that look in her eye, let them in. We've all been there and we can all help each other and learn from each others' experiences."

"You tend to look at people who've made a success of things as being different from you in some significant way; they come from a more advantaged background, they've got access to an amazing network or a big pot of cash... There's no reason why you can't do just as well, and you shouldn't ever feel intimidated by them. All you have to do is make a start, take each day at a time and don't worry so much about the bigger picture."

"Get something down on paper, even if that just means writing your ideas down, it's a start. Our first logo was a scribble, two little houses with smoke going from one chimney into the other, and with that we suddenly had something tangible. It wasn't designed by an advertising agency, it was just a little logo – but that was probably the first day that we had something real."

Ideas you can steal

Replication is nirvana
All too often great entrepreneurial ventures stumble when it comes to rolling them out because the entrepreneur themselves has been so instrumental in the initial success; how can you bottle the individual's passion and drive? So, unless you would be happy to see your venture remain a local affair or limited to what you can personally watch over, set about thinking how you can box it up, like Siobhan did, so that others can help it to grow.

Create it in your own image
There's nothing like knowing your target market inside out, and for Siobhan that wasn't difficult as netmums was created for mothers like her. Several people channel their social entrepreneurship to tackle an issue that they face themselves, and it's a pretty good way to make sure you know just what is needed. So, if you want to act but aren't quite sure in what way, look at an issue that you personally want to challenge.

Treat your sponsors as partners not just a cash pot
Siobhan has been expert in attracting corporate sponsors for netmums, and she's successful because she knows how the deal needs to work for them. It's not always enough to offer a company a bit of reflected glory by being seen next to your 'good cause'. Get strategic, think how a company might benefit from a multi-layered relationship like Huggies has with netmums. At the end of the day this will lead to a deeper and probably longer term relationship.

Jonathan Robinson

The Hub: an innovation 'incubator' comprising a 3,000 sq ft work-cum-social-space, where people with good ideas for the world can come together to work, meet and be creative.

Why he's here...

We chose Jonathan because quite simply he excites us. As you'll see from his story, his entrepreneurial activities have unfolded in a kind of spontaneous flow. One success leads to another, one event leads to a phone call which then stimulates yet another venture, and we find ourselves dying to find out 'what next?' from our youngest social entrepreneur. We see in him a rare ability to respond to a challenge and to take advantage of opportunity as well as a crucial fearlessness, whether it be in chasing cash or signing weighty contracts. Essentially, things happen when Jonathan takes on a project, and although The Hub is only in its formative years we have every faith that it will lead to great things.

?WHAT IF! UnLtd*

Who is Jonathan Robinson?

- Jonathan was born in 1979 and brought up in the Cumbrian hills close to Penrith. At 17 he won a scholarship to Atlantic College in Wales (a pioneering international sixth form focusing on global citizenship) where he took his International Baccalaureate.

- He studied social anthropology at Edinburgh University and graduated in 2002.

- He has been involved in several socially impactful projects since his teenage years, from taking an aid convoy to Bosnia during the war to writing a book on socially driven careers for the business publishers FT Prentice Hall.

The issues he confronted

- Along with a group of friends Jonathan felt that conventional and corporate careers dominated the market place, and that there was a lack of awareness of and support for different career paths, especially for those who want their work to tackle pressing world problems.

- Those who had decided to dedicate their lives to new ways of confronting the world's issues were having to do so from their bedrooms; there was no space for them to find the resources they needed for their project, nor to meet and share with other like-minded people in the same situation.

The solution he created

- The Hub opened its doors in January 2005. It offers time-based membership that works a bit like a mobile phone contract: people sign up on a tariff that suits them, ranging from pay-as-you-go to Hub 3,000 (minutes), to Hub Unlimited. Members get access to work and meeting spaces and all the gadgets that a social entrepreneur might need to get started. But more than this, The Hub is a space for people to come together to exchange ideas, experience and knowledge, for mutual benefit.

- Located in the heart of Islington, London, The Hub not only looks great, it also limits its impact on the environment through every aspect of its design and every material used: the desks are made from recycled cardboard and the striking red stoves which help heat the place use sawdust destined for landfill, thereby reducing CO_2 emissions.

Jonathan's story

How to create world leaders and social workers

One day when I was about 15 I found myself having a quick peek at my mum's copy of Country Living magazine. My eye had been drawn to this picture of some kids working on a farm, and it turned out to be at a school. I read the article and it seemed an interesting place called Atlantic College, where you go to a minimum number of lessons (I'm sure it was an illegally small number!) and every afternoon you were encouraged to abandon the classroom to go and do something useful in the community.

Beyond being light on lessons, the college was all about bringing together young people from about 70 countries around the world, and training them to foster international understanding. It was founded in 1962 by Kurt Hahn, the educational pioneer who also founded Outward Bound and numerous other forward thinking schooling initiatives. His big idea was that the college would turn out the next generation of world leaders, and if people had friends in other countries they would be less likely to go to war in the future. That was the rationale when Atlantic was set up during the cold war, but of course it doesn't actually turn out world leaders at all, it turns out social workers and people who start small and unusual projects. However that was their big idea and I think it was pretty instrumental in shaping my view of the world.

Atlantic was this rare hotbed of ideas. In some ways we were sheltered from the world, nestled on the coastline of South Wales, yet we were also exposed to its trials, tribulations, and opportunities in a big way; you might share a room with a guy who had escaped the genocide in Rwanda, and discuss climate change with a friend from Shanghai over breakfast. It was at Atlantic that I met Mark Hodge, Katy Marks, Yuill Herbert and many others that I've worked with on several projects and still do today. I think our first idealistic collaboration was to try and get the college to buy a wind turbine; in the process of proving the case we built a prototype in the form of an extremely long pole that shot up into the sky with a little propeller on the top. Getting it upright was seriously challenging, and when we finally did we were thrilled, but we woke up the next day to find it had fallen down almost killing a sheep, and the RAF were threatening to sue us for interfering with their local flight path. The wind turbine project didn't happen.

The college made me realise that there was some pretty compelling stuff out in the world to be concerned about. We learnt from each other how the world is connected, how fundamentally the stuff going wrong has some root causes. At the same time we learnt that conventional approaches to the world's problems were kind of lacking, and the people we should sympathise with in the charitable world were stuck pursuing solutions that didn't exude much creativity or imagination or radicalism. So that was us; a bunch of 18 and 19 year olds wanting to do something radical, imaginative and creative.

Being better than The Dome

We left Atlantic College in 1998 pretty fired up; there was the symbolic prospect of the millennium on the horizon and we felt we were in a kind of significant moment. The millennium seemed to us an opportunity for all sorts of people to be asking really big questions about their lives, values and work, and all the government was doing was building that travesty which is the Millennium Dome. So, one day soon after leaving college when a group of us were wandering down the South Bank and saw the Royal Festival Hall, we decided there and then to put on an event for the millennium. It would be an experience that would begin to shake up lots of peoples' thinking, including our own, about social issues and conventional solutions. So we landed up there and somehow managed to convince them to take a booking from us for two days the following year and we signed up a £20,000 contract; 'That's fine. See you in a year's time.'

Our plan was to fill it with some powerful thinkers, some amazing musicians, film, dance, poetry and debate, and we'd try and shake things up a bit. By the time our weekend came around in 1999 we had managed to persuade some of the world's leading players to be involved; Anita Roddick, Jon Snow and several Nobel Peace Prize Laureates. I'm not entirely sure how a bunch of 19 year olds attracted such figures; I guess it was our combination of being kind of cheeky and a bit humble all at the same time. We would get on the phone or send short, little messages on the fax machine and just hope for the best. When there was no response we would just persist and send it again and again. Once you got past the PA you'd begin to make some connections and it really was a wonderful experience to be talking to people that you've always really admired. We even managed to spend some time with the Dalai Lama in India to record a video message.

When the event came around I missed most of it being stuck backstage but it went really well, and there was a tremendous response from those who came along. But as good as it was, our immediate reaction was to want to just go back to normal life for a while. We'd spent the year in a space where we'd be calling Kate Adie or the Dalai Lama's office from payphones, only for the beeps to kick in half way through the conversation and the money to run out. We had started university by then and I had friends in halls having to accept messages from my Mum and Tony Blair's office in the same evening. It had got to a point where a few months out of that world was what we were looking for.

The alternative summit

But it was just a break we needed; our motivation was still very much there and The Royal Festival Hall was generating a few interesting opportunities, the most exciting of which was a phone call from the people organising the United Nations World Summit on Sustainable Development in Johannesburg for 2002. They were asking us to replicate the Royal Festival Hall gig in Johannesburg.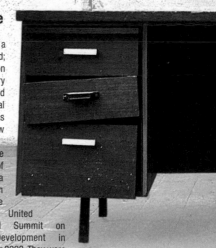

We were in the thick of studying at this point but managed to sneak off during reading week to check it out. We landed up in Johannesburg and very quickly realised that the corporate convention centres where they were going to host the summit just didn't do it for us; they were concrete edifices that represented the ironies of Johannesburg and the contradictions of our world and would totally undermine everything our event was about. So we abandoned that side of Johannesburg and against everyone's warnings that horrible things would befall us, decided to venture into Soweto to find out what people there made of this impending summit. We couldn't find anyone that knew anything about the world summit, but everyone knew about this other summit that was bang in the heart of Soweto. It was this little mountain that was covered in waste, a kind of park that people really feared venturing onto. There'd been horrible stories of rape and murder happening there and it had become a no-man's land, a very iconic but potentially beautiful piece of land just sticking out of the township.

The extraordinary characters that we met in the vicinity of this summit had been at the heart of the anti-apartheid movement and were now shifting their energy to community regeneration. For decades they been dreaming about how they could inhabit this piece of land and turn it into a space in which they could realise something positive and beautiful for Soweto with gardens and enterprise and music. At the time that we visited they were coming across all sorts of stumbling blocks; they couldn't get possession of the land, couldn't get any finance, the district council wasn't coping with the waste and it was just building up on this mountain, so a few of us took the decision that we really had to spend some time there to see what might happen and how we could help. We also felt there was a real connection between what these guys in Soweto were telling us they needed to make progress, and the global issues around progress and sustainable development that we wanted to be telling leaders at the UN summit.

Katy was the one in our team brave enough to spend close to 18 months in Soweto. She put her architecture degree to one side and spent her time working to surface in very quiet ways the aspirations and dreams of this community. We also spent some not so quiet times in wrangles with the people who owned the land and making pitches to people with money.

By the summer of 2002 and the UN summit the dream had been realised. The mountain was decorated with buildings made out of discarded glass bottles and car tyres, rocks had been carved into meeting spaces, and a water tower at the top of this mountain was turned into a light beacon. There were also half a dozen little social enterprises working around food, waste, music and film, and the community renamed the summit the Soweto Mountain of Hope. It's still very much alive to this day.

When the community started getting calls from Kofi Annan's people, John Prescott's people, and The Canadian Prime Minister was asking where his helicopter could land, we realised that it had

worked and we'd created a space that was intriguing enough that world leaders wanted to engage with it. We had three or four thousand World Summit delegates visit, and the special moment came when Kofi Annan, so moved by what he saw, scrapped his formal speech to speak from the heart. He said there was no point waiting for the UN summit to deliver because it had all happened down at what he called the real summit; this mountain in Soweto.

What about us?
After Soweto we all, and especially Katy, felt completely exhausted. We also ultimately needed to think seriously about our own futures and less about running around the world. It was now our final year at university and dawning on us was the fact that actually the biggest challenge was yet to come; in a few months time we'd be out facing the world of work, needing to earn some money to pay back the student loans, and the last thing we wanted was to get a job with a company that was going to be part of the problem rather than the solution.

Our response was to convince ourselves and a lot of other people that there was a different world out there to work within. It was at that time in university when you're constantly being seduced to go to fancy recruitment evenings hosted by big companies who crank up a particular idea of work and a particular idea of success that just didn't appeal. So we planned our own event to find out if anyone else was thinking like us; conventional career options are limited, and success is not being 'number one' and earning a wapping big salary. The event would open that debate, and it wouldn't just be for those who were aware of stuff like sustainability; our sights were firmly set on opening up the minds of those of our friends who didn't share our concerns about careers and companies that only add to the world's problems.

I remember being in a four hour traffic jam coming back from Dartmoor with one of our team, Lindsay Grey, when we finally realised how the event should work. We would set up a spoof company that was looking for bright young things to work in their corporation. It would be called Space PLC and be branded to look exactly like a 'serious player' in the world of work. We printed up fliers for a recruitment event and found ourselves completely oversubscribed, the website jammed and we had to turn people away at the door; so there was no turning back now! We 'head hunted' a provocateur for the night to be our CEO, and he described Space PLC as 'the company to work for, looking for the brightest and the best, and if you're male, tall, dark, handsome and see yourself as number one then your chances of working for us are even greater'.

As the evening wore on the pretence began to disintegrate and some people began to get a bit agitated about where we were taking them. But the vast majority were pretty gripped by the drama that was unfolding, and the evening progressed with our attempts to open up a debate about the most basic of questions, 'what do you really want to do with your life?', 'what change do you want to see in the world?'. We realised that we had done something a bit dangerous and we seriously pissed off the careers advice service, but the overall impact was positive; we made everyone who attended have conversations about careers that no-one else was facilitating. The challenge was then whether we could get around other universities before the whole show got closed down!

Gathering evidence
It was great stimulating that debate, but we realised that we were

missing quite a vital bit of the picture; where was our proof around this stuff? We'd asked people to write on the table cloths and I remember one person's just said 'prove it' in enormous letters. That really resonated for us, and we immediately set about finding evidence; as much for our own peace of mind as for the project. Beyond having a debate, was it really possible to roll out of university into the world and develop your own idea of work?

That proof came in the form of a book we wrote called Careers Un-Ltd. We found people that we admired, not the celebrities that we'd invited to the Royal Festival Hall, people like us but five or ten years later in life, who in various different contexts were and are making a confident stand. So there was Richard Reed from Innocent Smoothies, Renee Eliot from Planet Organic, Paul Kingsnorth from The Ecologist... These were people from all walks of life, from all over the country, and we told their stories so as to inspire us all to think beyond the limited confines of conventional careers. This wasn't about ethical careers, or certain jobs being OK and certain not being OK, this was about allowing a shift in mindset around how you approach pretty much any career opportunity.

Getting people out of their bedrooms

After the book came out we began to get lots of emails from people which threw up a whole new challenge. We discovered this whole set of people trying to realise good ideas from their bedroom; lonely, cut off from the world, not really fulfilling the potential of their ideas, and eating too much on their kitchen lunch breaks. So it dawned on us; what if these people could come together in the same physical space and have a place to hang out? Then maybe they could be more than the sum of the parts. Maybe we could begin to cultivate some powerful collaborations between people with all sorts of different expertise? So we began to imagine what it would take to create a habitat that would attract people and bring them together.

Around this time Etty Flanagan, another of our team was advised to meet a young lady for coffee. Quite unbelievably she came back saying this amazing person might help us with £1million to find a building that we could use for this new project. The rest of us couldn't believe it, and Etty and I set about a three month process to work with this extraordinary young lady to establish what might be possible.

So The Hub started to come to life, and at the same time as trying to get a grip of what it is, we were also trying to make sense of the property market which threw us all over the place. We got a bunch of friends together, gave them all digital cameras and a nice packed lunch, and sent them off in every possible direction around London. They'd come back at the end of the day with another umpteen potential interesting sites for us to go and visit. In the end we saw something close to 100 buildings at a time when we were all meant to be working to earn a living. We came very close to buying the perfect building, but it was more like two and a bit million pounds, so we had to work seriously hard approaching other investors to make up the shortfall. But we got the money and had our hearts firmly set, then on the day of exchange it all went pear-shaped. A last minute survey said that the building had a chance of falling down in 20 years' time and so the deal fell apart in those final hours.

That was a big blow and we all got pretty close to giving up. Then I had one of those random meetings; I was sitting in The Candid Arts Café in Islington which is part of a huge warehouse building, and I got into one of those conversations where you're a bit bored

and kind of hoping it might end soon. It turned out to be the guy who looked after the whole building. He told us he might let us rent the top floor. There were chemicals all over the floor and pigeon shit everywhere so a few health and safety issues, but we agreed that we'd take it on.

We had lost the vast majority of our £2million finance overnight when the big building fell through. But now we were going to rent so it was a different proposition for investors; it's not about putting money into a property, it's about asking people to invest in a business, a business that they didn't quite understand and that had never been done before. So finding funding was a different challenge on a different scale; but we raised £150,000 to realise the dream.

We set about a six month process of regenerating the place from a derelict shell into something that is beautifully designed, works functionally to achieve our ambitions of a communal space, and has as little impact on the planet as possible. We had a strong sense that we didn't just want to bring in an architect, we wanted to invite the very people that were interested in inhabiting the space to come together to design how it would be. So, we gave 30 of them some chalk and essentially set about a collaborative design process. We wanted to create a space that wasn't like anything any of us had experienced before; not like a professional office, not a club, not your living room, not a bar, but in some ways combining the best of all of these.

Making sure we didn't trash the planet in the process threw up some really interesting challenges. We found some stoves that we really love because they not only create that cosy fireside atmosphere, they also reduce 80% of CO_2 emissions by burning sawdust that would have landed up in landfill. But you can't burn fuel in London so we had a bit of a battle with the local authority, as we tried to convince them we had the best reason to break an environmental rule.

In terms of users we wanted to create a place that was buzzing and alive with all sorts of characters coming and going, so we borrowed from mobile phone tariffs to invent our own time-based membership. You can sign up to at different levels; Hub 3,000, Hub 6,000, Hub Unlimited, giving you different access in terms of minutes per month. That has helped create a really dynamic community of over 100 members and many thousands of visitors over the last nine months.

We kind of stumbled into the opening, again rather exhausted. We'd taken on a bit of an insane challenge to turn a dilapidated space into something beautiful and functional in next to no time. We'd also overspent; rather predictably for a building project our ambitions had cost us more than we thought they would. But nine months on it is doing much better than we expected financially. It's a stable business model and we're not having to beg or borrow money from anyone. We can also afford to pay the core team a salary which is great because since university we've all done all sorts of jobs to keep us personally afloat; working in a motorway service station doing the washing up was about my most glamorous way of paying the rent.

Anyone for Brazil?

Since opening there's been an extraordinary amount of interest from around the country and around the world. People have spotted that there's something interesting going on here that could really work for them, whether they're in Sao Paulo, New York, Johannesburg, Glasgow... There is something about what we've created in London that has really caught their attention, and our challenge is to work out how we replicate whilst still maintaining what is great about The Hub.

On one level, this place is about something very basic. People are compelled to come here because we provide the tools that we all need to get stuff done; phones that work, desks, chairs... But what really interests us is that other level which is more about the intangibles; what happens when people who have been locked in their bedrooms or in jobs they hate get to share and exchange with like-minded people; what is the value created when a lawyer finds himself next to the local film-maker, a computer programmer, or a fashion designer? I sometimes think about collaborations that happen here in terms of relationships; you see things that look a bit like a one-night stand, all a bit fleeting and everyone gets what they want rather quickly and they never see each other again; then you get more enduring relationships when two people really hit it off and embark on a joint venture together. It's that intangible value that we're increasingly interested in working with in various ways.

It's something to do with the mystery of connections. We believe that often the most meaningful connections and some of the most powerful outcomes happen without being planned. It's the magic of serendipity. This is the stuff that complexity scientists describe as emergence. It's about the dynamic mix of old and new world views, of chaos and order, of top-down and bottom up and of leadership and participation such that really surprising and powerful things start happening.

So The Hub is interested in creating the conditions for emergence. This is about creating the lightest possible structure such that the talents of the people who hang out here become liberated and applied in powerful ways.

My call to arms

"Right now, this morning I need a lawyer because I've just heard that a bunch of entrepreneurs, not driven by any social objectives are opening something pretty identical to what we do in central London and they've even called it 'The Hub'. So I need to get on their case and try and stop them ruining our social brand."

"Long-term, we'd love people with great ideas for the world to get in touch so that we can maintain the flow of people meeting people."

My top tips

"Break the rules. Rise to opportunities that allow you to change the rules of the game. For example when we were looking for a publisher for our little book, we didn't do the conventional thing. We wrote a two line cheeky little letter to an editor at one of the world's biggest publishers and it seems that she couldn't resist picking up the phone to work out 'what's going on here?'. So rather than our synopsis landing up the bin, I found myself being invited out for lunch making the case face-to-face."

"Make yourself indispensable to the person that you most admire. Whether that's Jon Snow or the fashion designer that lives next door, don't go begging for help, prove to them that they need you!"

I think we're speaking to powerful trends in the wider world around the disintegration of conventional ways of organising. No longer is the most effective way to get things done about top-down power and deployment; the organisational form for the future is one centred around networks. That's exactly the kind of organisation we're generating here with all these independent, autonomous agents, driven by a strong sense of what's wrong in the world, wanting to do something about it, and coming together to form a fluid, but potentially very powerful network. It makes things happen. It's that cliché about all these disparate people adding up to something altogether more powerful than the sum of their parts.

Ideas you can steal

Challenge the conventional voluntary sector solutions

If we achieve one thing from writing this book, it would be to make people understand that conventional approaches to the world's issues are not foolproof. People are reluctant to question charities and NGOs because they are seen to be doing great work, but unchallenged they will never innovate or improve. Jonathan and his friends took this challenging stance as their starting point and it's given them the freedom to do great things.

Make connections not just appeals

Speak to the great and the good in person wherever possible; don't settle for a PA because you'll never build a connection. People, however important, will help, but only if you can engage them personally in your project and your team.

Build it and they will come

People respond to actual outcomes and physical realities, not paper presentations. Jonathan and the team had thousands of world leaders come to see their work in Soweto; a talking shop simply wouldn't have had that appeal.

Be provocative

There are plenty of conferences and get-togethers for those concerned with social change, and they're fairly comfortable affairs. The world needs shaking up, and that's about how we debate things as well as what we do about them. Don't be afraid to change the rules, flip the dynamic and make people feel just a little uncomfortable; that way we might just get some new solutions.

Colin Crooks

Green-Works: prevents thousands of tonnes of unwanted office furniture from going to landfill every year by repairing it and redistributing to charities, schools and start-up organisations. Green-Works also provides opportunities to long-term unemployed and disabled people.

Why he's here...

Take a walk around a Green-Works depot and you are a world away from the traditional charity set-up. Service is everything and quality is paramount, but the overarching idea is to prevent anything that comes through their door from going to landfill. Green-Works is an example of how you can marry a mission with a competitive business. What also impresses us is the way Colin's model delivers social impact in every direction; what they bring in, what they send out, and who they employ. There was previously no viable solution for businesses to clear their offices, and now Green-Works is growing rapidly in terms of finance, the services they can offer, their client rota, and therefore the positive impact they're having on the environment; Colin just seems to have got it right.

Who is Colin Crooks?

Colin was born in 1961 and grew up in a small village near Portsmouth. He moved to London when he was 18 and has worked in a number of jobs including being a window cleaner and a policeman.

At 23 Colin became a mature student and studied History, Politics and Middle Eastern History at Royal Holloway University, London. He later went on to take an MSc in Environmental Conservation at Greenwich University.

Colin set up Green-Works in 2000.

The issues he confronted

Over 100 million tonnes of waste is dumped in landfill sites every year in England and Wales. Landfill space is now at a premium and gas emission from the sites is becoming a growing environmental issue.

The UK recycles only 10% of its unwanted goods compared to 50% in some parts of Europe; the rest, despite often being in good condition, is put in landfill.

Because businesses are moving offices more frequently, an increasing amount of unwanted furniture is being generated. Traditional recycling schemes are expensive and time-consuming so businesses are reluctant to move away from landfill.

Many charities, schools, and non-profit organisations really need decent quality, low-cost furniture.

The solution he created

Green-Works clear offices before they are refurbished. 100% of the furniture they process is diverted from landfill. If the donated item is in good condition it is sold on at affordable rates to a charity or community group. If it is unusable it is broken down and the component materials either sent directly for recycling or 'chipped' for use as refuse derived fuel.

Where possible Green-Works train and employ disabled people and people who have been out of work for long periods.

Colin's story

Timing is everything

I've always been an environmentalist; I remember when I was eight, taking some newspapers down to the local recycling centre with my scout group, getting some money for them, and thinking, ooh that's cool, I like that! I just can't stand the idea of waste – which means my shed is full of old screws and bits and pieces. But I'm sure they'll come in handy one day.

Having graduated from university I found myself in a very strange position where I was too qualified. I think a lot of organisations want people who are mouldable and because I'd been working for the previous seven years I didn't fit that bill. So, I started by managing a window cleaning business at Canary Wharf. Then one day, I bumped into a friend whom I hadn't seen for ages; a week later he rang me up and said, 'You're really into the environment, why don't you come to my company and show us how to

In 1994, the price of paper collapsed suddenly – there was a 34% drop in price overnight. I was very lucky, as I managed to sell the business to another company who needed to increase their volumes as prices fell.

Going with the flow

I guess becoming a consultant was a natural progression: I'd learnt a lot about all the pitfalls that you inevitably face trying to set up a whole new system and make it work, and my MSc in Environmental Conservation consolidated this knowledge. So I started offering advice to people on an ad hoc basis; after a few years this grew into a consultancy offering a range of environmental management services for mostly London-based businesses. But I wasn't finding consultancy satisfying; often you find yourself producing a really long report which you know

recycle?'. So I bought a van for £400 and drove round to all my friends' offices and got paper from them and organised a Saturday morning run, which was fun. That grew within about six months to become a full-time business called Paper Cycle, which ended up employing about 15 people running three vehicles.

A lot of the success of the business was in the timing: in the early nineties recycling was taking off; there was a big market for it but many of the businesses which were offering recycling services weren't particularly big on customer service. The people running those businesses were mainly market traders with trucks; they weren't sales or marketing people. Nor am I particularly, but what I did find is that if you give quality service, for example if you say you'll be there on Tuesday and you turn up on Tuesday, it makes a big difference. It's not rocket science, but it is the little things that make customers loyal. I also found that going that little bit further, like writing to them and telling them how many trees they'd saved last month was a big incentive, too; it promotes a feel good factor, which is really important.

they're only going to put on their shelf so they can tick a box to say it's been done, and never look at again. It's frustrating when you don't see any improvements.

And then, rather like that chance phone call, another life changing thing happened which expanded my horizons somewhat: Gateshead Council called me looking for advice on developing a recycling scheme for old washing machines and fridges. For some reason they'd heard I was an expert! Obviously I didn't have a clue, but being a consultant meant I had plenty of contacts so I did know who to talk to; so I set about finding out what we could do, and got the job.

That led to a new project being developed, called Renew North East which was hugely successful. It trains mainly young unemployed men to fix washing machines and fridges which then get passed on at low-cost to people and families on low incomes. So everyone wins: the men get jobs and learn new skills that will set them up for the future, and the public gets a warranted, clean and fully operational washing machine for £90.

Although at that stage I didn't really fully appreciate the term social enterprise, Renew North East was in many ways a classic example of one: everyone working for us had come off the dole and all the money that we were raising we were ploughing back into the business. When I started finding out more about what social enterprise was about, it all began to fit perfectly – I thought 'this is fantastic, it's exactly what I'm doing'.

Solving a conundrum

Then one day I started thinking about all this furniture that my clients in London were complaining about and I couldn't help them with: they were disposing of hundreds of desks at a time from office moves, but the second hand dealers only wanted the best

van, got a volunteer driver in. At first, we either took the furniture straight to the customer, to the community group or school, or put it into a lock-up garage which was lent to us rent-free for a few months. The garage route was a disaster because of course it all went mouldy and was unusable.

Feeling in the dark

The first year was really about just testing the water. We needed to see how much of a need there was and whether people would actually pay for it. So we charged the client a fee for collection and the recipient a fee for the furniture. We didn't charge the charities very much because we couldn't store the furniture or clean it up as we didn't have any facilities, so it was really just a token fee to cover our costs.

ones. They knew that schools would love them but when you're moving office and need to get shot of furniture quickly, it's not realistic to start delivering it all around the place. It was crazy because through my consultancy I could help them get every single possible consumable recycled, from CDs to plastic cups to cardboard to toner cartridges, no problem. We could even get some of their IT equipment recycled. But there simply wasn't any money in recycling furniture; it just didn't make economic sense because the chipboard is worthless and it takes a lot of labour to strip the metal components off the furniture.

So I thought that perhaps that was a gap that could be filled by a social enterprise; perhaps we could try taking some of this furniture, a lot of which was really good stuff, and put it to good use. And that's exactly what we did; we just tried it. I was running my consultancy three days a week which wasn't exactly bringing in a huge amount of money but it was paying the mortgage. And a couple of days a week I worked on setting up Green-Works, making calls and trying to get people interested. I rented the odd

We turned over £2,000 that year and I didn't get paid. It wasn't a lot of money but it did prove that fundamentally there was something there. So the following year we put the prices up a bit, approached things in a more systematic way, and managed to find a proper warehouse, which we were offered rent-free for six months. That was a big lift and it began to feel like things were taking off.

Desperate times

I managed to get hold of enough furniture to fill up the warehouse and the van was fairly busy out on collections, but the furniture just wasn't moving; we couldn't get the customers to come to the warehouse to collect it. We tried leaflet drops to charities in the Greenwich area but there just seemed to be no interest. I knew we had to do something dramatic because after six months we'd have to start paying rent and that would break us. So desperate times called for desperate measures! I literally emailed every single friend and colleague I had (I was a local councillor at the time) who might be interested or who might know someone who might be interested in low-cost office furniture. 110 emails and a week later, the warehouse had emptied.

Word had got around so fast; we had people who'd received the email from a friend of a friend of a friend of a friend, turning up saying, 'I hear you've got some cheap furniture for charities, is that right?' and they just went in and took it! The next week we filled the warehouse up and emptied it again. That was the magic turning point for us. It proved that customers would pay us for a service; the charities were lining up to come and get the furniture. So the model was working, it was brilliant. That was the point where things really took off.

Needing a leg up

Then in early 2002 I injured my knee quite severely and had to go into hospital in March. Not being a very good planner, I'd only realised by February that I didn't have anyone to run the business, no-one to drive the van, load and unload the furniture. I did have a volunteer driver but I'd been doing a lot of the driving as well and it was too much for one person alone. At the time we had a big contract with a client to clear their building, amounting to about 40 desks every fourth weekend, and I didn't know how we were going to cope. So I took a punt and recruited someone to run the show while I was out of action. Chris is still with us today. He had two days to learn the ropes before I said, 'Right I'm off to hospital, over to you.' He was only 23! A week later he came to see when I was in bed at home with a big plaster on my leg and updated me on what he had done and how it was all going. And there were no problems - he was brilliant.

In those days we were jack of all trades: we had to learn how to be porters, drivers, salesmen. And it was bloody hard work. But we had some volunteers helping out and there was this fantastic energy, with everyone mucking in.

Developing partnerships

A lot of organisations get charged a penalty if they're moving offices and the furniture isn't moved by the time they leave, and to speed up the process they hire out companies to sort it all out for them. So we started to develop partnerships with those companies that were providing the manpower and the trucks for the moves, and we got the jobs together.

We are more expensive than standard clearance companies because our approach is more labour intensive. Warehousing furniture rather than sending it to a landfill site is an ongoing expense and we have to cover those costs. But people are clearly willing and able, to pay for it; we show them what their furniture could do if they just paid a little bit more for our service, rather than trashing it.

We recycle absolutely everything now; if we can't sell something we'll break it down into recyclable components. Sometimes we even send stuff to Africa. We've recently sent several loads to the Sudan, to help set up a dental hospital, and to charities in the Gambia. At the moment we're working with a major corporate client to develop furniture exports to Ghana.

Playing with the big boys

In May 2002 a Christian charity, First Fruit, approached us, wanting to create jobs for homeless people. I had this vision of a massive warehouse, with everyone working together, transforming furniture and selling it on. Then shortly afterwards, HSBC asked us to help come up with a solution for their massive office move into Canary Wharf from over 20 sites across central London. They had 3,000 tonnes of redundant furniture and didn't want to put it into landfill. So we combined the two problems and managed to come up with this brilliant solution: we signed a contract with HSBC to take all their redundant office equipment off their hands and opened up an enormous warehouse in Silvertown, east London. Within the first three months of opening we'd taken in 1,000 tonnes of furniture; over half of it was sold on to charities and the rest was recycled. HSBC was totally delighted. We never looked back.

We work on a basis of complete transparency; our corporate clients pay a premium for our services so it's important that they get the recognition from the charities that they donate to. Another reason for that is there can potentially be a clash between the companies' and the charities' aims: for example, we might have a tobacco company sending us furniture that could end up in a cancer charity and we understand that that may not be acceptable. So we label all the furniture clearly with details of where it came from.

Going that bit further

We now have four warehouses, employing up to about 80 people. Of those, 40 are employed by us and 40 are taken on by franchisees. The franchisees are all social enterprises which support the training and development of unemployed people. There is one in Paisley called Kibble which cares for young people who have been expelled from school and need a secure learning environment. The Green-Works approach is perfect for them: for these young people to learn new skills, to completely renovate an old

desk and then sell it on to a school which really needs it, is a great confidence boost. We get them involved in all aspects of the business, from monitoring the stock as it comes in and goes out, to dealing directly with clients.

Big plans

Looking forward I'd like us to expand; we need to be nationwide. I'd also like us to be able to install a complete recycled office, the whole thing. We are building the basis for this, we can now supply carpets, waste paint and can do soft furnishings and fitted cupboards, so we're getting closer to that goal every month. The big step after that is being able to install the office, which would mean a huge training programme and would provide more opportunities for our people to develop and more roles for them to grow into; for example they could become fitters and project managers, etc. – the possibilities are endless.

Ideas you can steal

Muck in

Colin and his team generated this fantastic energy by everyone pulling together in order to get things up and running. They put in long hours and a lot of physical labour and although it wasn't easy, it was only through everyone pitching in that got the job done and kept the clients sweet. In the early days in particular, that's sometimes what you have to expect.

Learn as you go along

Not being an expert in a particular area didn't stop Colin from having a go and learning as he went along. A lot of his success can be put down to not being afraid of not knowing; when he didn't have a clue about recycling old washing machines he went and found out, and that new knowledge led to him setting to setting up a whole new organisation.

Remember your friends

People can often overlook the value of friends and relatives when they get in a sticky situation; often that's because they get so stuck in 'business mode' that they don't think to call on people who are outside that sphere. Friends can be really useful; and even those you think won't be able to help may know someone who can. When in doubt, get out the little black book; Colin did and it changed things for him dramatically.

Tim Smit

The Eden Project: one of the UK's foremost visitor attractions, consisting of two vast greenhouses in a disused clay pit, based in Cornwall. Eden explores man's relationship with nature, and highlights the need for sustainability in modern life through what is described as a 'living theatre of plants and people'.

Tim's dream was to build the eighth wonder of the world in a disused clay pit in Cornwall. Not only did he achieve this dream, he did it in such a way that the values of social entrepreneurship, sustainability and citizenship are made clear to the millions who visit. Eden challenges perceptions of science, nature and environmentalism and in so doing appeals to the 'non-converted', that vast majority of the UK that is all too often left unmoved by mainstream environmental campaigns and charities. Eden is quite simply a marvel; one of the world's most pioneering social enterprises, the fourth most popular (paid for) attraction in the UK, and a treasure that we think will inspire generations to come.

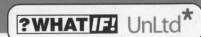

Who is Tim Smit?

- Tim was born in Holland in 1954, but educated in Britain. He studied Archaeology and Anthropology at Durham University.

- He spent the first half of his career in the music industry as a composer and producer in both rock and opera, achieving seven platinum and gold discs in ten years.

- In 1987 Tim moved to Cornwall where he met John Nelson and together they restored the Lost Gardens of Heligan, which has been voted the Nation's Favourite Garden.

- Tim's work at the Eden Project has led to him receiving countless awards and honorary doctorates. He was featured on the ITV series This is Your Life in 2001, and awarded a CBE in 2002. Tim's book, The Lost Gardens of Heligan, was Illustrated Book of the Year at the 1997 British Book Awards and headed the Sunday Times bestseller list for several months. The ten part documentary of the same name won the Garden Documentary of the Year Award in 1998. Tim has subsequently published Heligan: Secrets Lost in Silence (1998) and The Heligan Vegetable Bible, co-written with Philip McMillan Browse (2000). His book Eden is also a best-seller.

The issues he confronted

- Only 3 million people in Britain are signed up to environmental causes or organisations; 53 million people are not.

- The average wage in Cornwall is 28% below that of the UK at large; Cornwall is the poorest county in the UK and one of the poorest regions in Europe. This meant that Eden was the only UK project of its kind not to receive any county level funding, and that despite being a charity has had to secure bank loans as finance.

The solution he created

- The Eden Project physically consists of two vast biomes (basically greenhouses) housing plants, crops and landscapes from the humid tropics and warm temperate regions of the world, and an 'outdoor biome' which is a temperate landscape. This is situated in a disused clay pit just outside St Austell in Cornwell.

- Around 500 full-time staff are now employed, all of whom were recruited locally, many were previously unemployed, and 40% are over 50 years in age. The project has also created nearly 2,000 full-time jobs in the wider South-West area.

- Over 7 million people have visited Eden so far, one third of whom are new to Cornwall.

- Eden generates £150million a year outside of its own business, for the Cornish economy; this is a bigger contribution than the whole of the European budget for the county.

- Interactive displays, workshops, art, music and performance are a big part of the Eden experience and are designed to appeal to a broad cross-section of people, especially those who are new to environmental issues.

- Eden is also a major educational scientific and environmental resource and works in partnership with local schools, colleges, universities, international scientists and artists.

Tim's story

Being English...

I'm a Dutchman by birth, although I'm now an adopted English bloke and one of the few things I hate about England is its desire to always preserve and conserve the past at any cost; this to me is very unhealthy. To me it doesn't come from a real belief that the past is somehow a better place, it's a sign of fear of the future, and a fear of change and innovation. Innovation is a very funny word. In business and in government these days you hear all this jargon surrounding innovation, like 'joined-up thinking', 'thinking out of the box', 'cutting edge'... I don't think we need to live too close to the edge; for me, innovation is something which comes from inside, in a way that is rather ordinary.

Not all rock 'n' roll

After studying Archaeology and Anthropology I worked as an archaeologist for a while in north-east England, and then joined a rock 'n' roll band. The band made a lot more money than archaeology, so I went to London and did rock 'n' roll for a while. I actually did rock 'n' roll and blues and opera, but after a time I'd had enough of London and I'd had enough of the music business. I didn't like most of the people I met and I didn't like the industry, so I moved down to Cornwall. There I met a man who'd just inherited a very large estate called Heligan Manor and he invited me to come up and see the place; it was a completely overwhelming experience. It felt like coming home; after 45 minutes of hacking my way through the gardens I'd decided to give up the music industry. That was it; boof, I knew what I wanted to do. I wanted to restore that magical place to all its former glory, and to open it up to the public so that anyone and everyone could enjoy its beauty. Today, Heligan is the most visited private garden in Britain, but when I found it, it had been asleep for 70 years.

No such thing as bad publicity?

I learnt a lot of lessons in that garden, the first being never underestimate the power of the media. I knew that in order to make the garden popular it would have to get some press, so I persuaded the BBC to come along and do a slot on Gardeners'

World. The coverage was fantastic, but there was one mistake; they forgot to mention that we weren't yet open to the public. So the next day the little old ladies from goodness knows where turned up in a coach expecting to be shown around. The day after that six coaches turned up; it was a complete pig's ear because the major work was still going on. On the third day my colleague John said, 'Why don't we rip the toilet out of the Portaloo and we'll have a ticket office?' In our first year we had 40,000 visitors when we hadn't even intended to be open. They'd arrive and ask about an area of the gardens we hadn't yet reached, so we'd give them a stick and tell them to go and find out what was down there. We had people not only paying to come visit an unfinished garden, but also helping us to do the work.

I remember the day we appointed our first head gardener. Two coaches of visitors arrived, one filled with well-to-do ladies from a flower arranging society, and the other with willing hands from the British Trust for Conservation Volunteers (BTCV). Unfortunately the coaches came in at times opposite to when we'd expected them; the ladies' coach came in first and the head gardener greeted them with, 'Hoy, you lot, out!' He marched them to the nursery garden and had them clearing it in no time. When the conservation volunteers turned up they got a guided tour and a cup of tea; they had a fantastic day and swore they'd come back any time. Incredibly though, the ladies had a great time too. I learnt from this that people actually really want to get involved. Those people who came that first year of Heligan remain friends of the project to this day because they were involved in trying to work out the puzzle of the place.

Something primitive

I also discovered that people are fascinated by things that grow out of the ground; not only the plants but also the actual living side to the soil. I don't know what its beauty or its attraction is but it fascinates people, and we're not talking about an earthy Country Living lifestyle choice here; it's something that is very, very primitive. I think that's what lies behind the beauty and the success of the Eden Project. Eden is a tremendous symbol of 'something'; everybody thinks it is just about plants, but it isn't. We took the most derelict place you could imagine because we wanted to symbolically give it life, and we chose plants because they're common to all people; I guess we wanted something that was a canvas on which to tell human stories. So you see it's not just about the plants, it's about the human relationship with plants and with nature.

One of the great quotes that I often use comes from CS Lewis: 'While science may lead you towards the truth, only the imagination can give you meaning'. One of the problems we have as humans is that we need stories to give truths meaning and make people change their behaviour; at Eden I think we have created a story to do just that.

The eighth wonder of the world

So with Heligan under our belts and using all the energy and inspiration of that project we turned our minds to Eden and hatched a plan to quite literally build the eighth wonder of the world. We went round various people asking for money and I would say: 'We're going to build the eighth wonder of the world, and it'll be absolutely fantastic.' Dead silence. Eventually they said, 'Look, if we give you £25,000 will you go away?'. We got bits and pieces of money after that, and then we went to the Millennium Commission. They liked the idea, but said we'd need to get an architect of 'international stature' on board, so we went to Nicholas Grimshaw who'd designed the Waterloo International Terminal: 'We've got some good news and some bad news: the good news is we'd like to offer you the chance to build the eighth wonder of the world, the bad news is we can't pay you.' He said he'd think about and off we went back to Cornwall. The next day the phone rang and it was Nick: 'I talked to all my guys and they're all in'. For the next 18 months probably the finest design team in the world worked on Eden for absolutely nothing.

So things were falling into place, but this was still a hell of an undertaking, and I remember a friend saying to me very early on, 'Tim this is going to be the ruin of you, your reputation is going to be lying in tatters.' This worried me for a few days, until my son reminded me that I didn't have a reputation to lose, so what was

I worried about? Some consolation! Then we did something rather unusual; staring the task of the build square in the face we got the design team and the constructors in a room and said, 'If you were me standing here now, what question would you be asking in order to make this team build the project on time and on budget?'. About five hours later, they came up with a suggestion. We followed their idea, and what do you know, we built the first phase on time, on budget, and without one single major argument.

Industrial choreography

On the 17 October 1998 two things happened; we bought the pit, and 400 miles away in Warrington a guy called Jerry didn't retire. Jerry had worked for the big construction firm Sir Robert McAlpine for years and was about to pick up his retirement papers when he heard that they'd won the Eden contract. That moment he decided not to retire but to take on our job as his final challenge, the one he could tell his grandchildren about. On the morning of the 18th October it started to rain, and it carried on raining for 134 days. In January the following year, 43 million gallons of water poured into

the bottom of the site, and the hillside which was to provide the foundations for our visitor centre turned to a hopeless red blancmange that slid down the side of the pit. At that point a knighthood and a million pounds in your back pocket wouldn't have mattered; what mattered was that you knew the right people, and I knew Jerry. So I called him up and said, 'Jerry, we're fucked'. He said, 'Leave it to me', and he got together 60 of the toughest guys you've ever met and a load of machinery. For six weeks there was this incredibly humbling sight of the most fantastic industrial choreography. These guys worked round the clock to rebuild our foundations and put in the drains, and today when it pisses with rain, the water flows clear as a mountain stream allowing us to recycle every drop.

In May of the following year we had an opening party. I arranged it so that Jerry would arrive after everyone else, and when he turned up I got up on stage: 'Jerry, you're here under false pretences. You've been voted the guy without whom Eden would not have happened, and I know you wanted to tell your family and your grandchildren about this project.' Unbeknown to him his whole family was there, all hiding in the kitchen behind the stage, and one by one they came out. Jerry's a big guy, but suddenly he had tears pouring down his face. I could just about handle that, but when the 60 tough guys who'd literally dug us out of the shit, started sniffling too, I'm afraid I couldn't handle it either. That really set the tone for the Eden project!

Beyond environmentalists...

So we now have this incredible site exhibiting groundbreaking architecture and telling the story of plants and humans from around the world; our challenge is attracting those people for whom environmentalism isn't a big pull, the 53 odd million people mentioned in the introduction who haven't yet involved themselves in the debate. One way we do this is to host the Eden Sessions throughout August; four nights when some of the biggest names in music perform on an incredible stage in front of the biomes. We can't be just a place for gardeners and nature lovers, and the Eden Sessions is just one of the things that we do to challenge the rest of society and get them asking questions.

...and beyond plants

Eden is also about our relationship to where we live and how we can make our commercial activities ethical. We employ 500 staff from the local community and we put about £150million a year into the county economy which is more than the entire European budget for Cornwall. 90% of all the food we use and sell comes from Cornish producers, and around 60% of everything we sell in our shop is locally sourced (remarkable considering that film and books, among our biggest sellers, are not made in Cornwall). We also offer long-term contracts to our suppliers to afford them more financial stability and confidence to build their businesses up. We also help those suppliers to find work with other companies so that they're not dependent on us; this means that if Eden were to take a downturn we'd be less likely to take lots of local businesses down with us.

Being a grown up

When Eden got to a certain size our Chair of Trustees felt we needed a more mature 'staff management system', which meant introducing things like key performance indicators (KPIs). I've always thought these practices were unnecessary if you only employed the right people in the first place, but I followed his lead and set about designing and implementing Eden's management system. Our trick was to design something within this business style framework, but that was totally unique to us and that would drive the qualities that we wanted at Eden; we created KPIs Eden style: over a certain period of time you must read two books that are completely outside your interests; you must go to films, concerts and plays and then review them for your colleagues; you must make someone else's wish come true in a way which is totally unexpected by the other person; and every three weeks we work at night because people have great ideas at night. These aren't a voluntary code of conduct, they're written into everyone's contract. At first glance they might look frivolous, or just about making Eden a fun place to work, but they are rooted in business sense: we want our staff to be creative so we encourage them to be constantly experiencing new things; we have people work at night because that's when they relax enough to bring in their 'outside work' experiences into play. Despite my original misgivings what we've created has become a highly effective way to get the best out of our people, whilst staying true to what the Eden Project is all about.

Let's be angry

I know it sounds soppy, but what Eden has proven to me is a belief that together we can change the world into a better place. The trouble is that we say we should be doing it for our children and our children's children, but that's a cop out. We should be doing it for us. We should be angry about the things we don't like; we should be angry that as a race we abuse the resources around us, that we don't care for our environment, that we have no proper understanding of what a sustainable future looks like, that commerce is all too often unethical. Eden proves that all these things are surmountable and that human behaviour can change. If we get angry now then maybe 1,000 years from now, people will remember this as the time when we grabbed life by the throat and said, 'we can make it better'.

Ideas you can steal

Preach to the unconverted

By presenting a traditionally stuffy subject like conserving the environment in a modern, interesting way Tim has captured the public's imagination. He has challenged and stimulated people, inviting them to look at issues in a new light, but at the same time has kept it relevant to people's everyday experiences. As social entrepreneurs we can easily just sell or campaign to those who already believe in this stuff, but the big wins - the major social impact - will come by converting those sections of society who aren't already engaged.

Stories make people change behaviour

Every great social entrepreneur we've come across has been able to clearly tell the story of what they're trying to achieve. Not only can Tim tell his own inspiring story; he has created a story through Eden which informs people about sustainability, about humans and nature, and about a better way of doing things. Stories are the way to bring people with you, and far more powerful more than any mission statement or presentation.

Engage the wider team

Whether you're working with kids, businesses or refugees, engage your stakeholders. Their insight will help to devise a better solution, plus their involvement in the design process will make them far more committed when the work starts. When Tim was faced the daunting task of starting to build Eden he simply asked the construction team to stand in his shoes and think what they would do. Working from their own plan that team proceeded to get the job done on time and within budget; surely a miracle in the building trade, and one that shows the power of stakeholder engagement.

People who get dirty stay involved

Having the flower arranging ladies cut paths into the Heligan undergrowth meant that they were involved, they felt a part of the project, and that they would have a lasting loyalty to the project. People want to help and they want to participate. Don't be afraid to ask; you'll get loads more back if you give people a role.

A full story

Tim doesn't just pay lip-service to the environmental message that he puts across; the project employs local people and uses local resources whenever possible. It's complete; it walks, talks and breathes social entrepreneurship.

Jordan Kassalow

Our International Story

The Scojo Foundation: works in the developing world to select, train and equip women entrepreneurs to provide communities with local eye care and affordable reading glasses.

Why he's here...

Scojo is not only an entrepreneurial venture in itself, it also generates entrepreneurship as its distribution method. We think this will ensure The Scojo Foundation is financially sustainable, and that it will generate economic impact well beyond the core mission to distribute glasses. We've also seen few better examples of how for-profit and non-profit enterprises can benefit each other when put side by side; resources are shared and each set of staff become infused with the best 'the other side' has to offer.

Jordan is also our one international social entrepreneur. We thought it would be good to get a bit of a global comparison, plus the story of The Scojo Foundation is quite simply too good to miss out on; true social entrepreneurship working in America and the developing world, and very definitely changing the world.

?WHAT IF! UnLtd*

Who is Jordan Kassalow?

Jordan grew up in the suburbs of New York City, and studied Optometry in Boston. It was as a student that he first started travelling in the developing world to deliver eye care.

He completed his Masters in Public Health at Johns Hopkins University, Baltimore, and went on to serve as the Director of the River Blindness Program at Helen Keller International in New York. This led to him work extensively on public health issues in Africa, India and Latin America.

Jordan established the Global Health Program at the Council on Foreign Relations where he served for five years as an Adjunct Senior Fellow in Global Health, and he serves on several boards.

The issues he confronted

1.6 million people in the developing world lack proper eye care.

On average it's 50km to the nearest eye clinic in developing countries.

The solution he created

The Scojo Foundation was launched in 2001 alongside the for-profit business Scojo Vision.

The Foundation exists to: develop markets for reading glasses for people at the base of the economic pyramid; select, train, equip and fund local entrepreneurs to establish new businesses that sell reading glasses; provide high-quality, affordable reading glasses for their programs; bring reading glasses and referral services directly to the customer at the village level; conduct innovative and locally relevant social marketing campaigns to raise awareness about blurry up close vision.

There are three income streams for The Scojo Foundation: Scojo Vision donates 5% of its profits; revenue from the sale of glasses to entrepreneurs; and conventional fundraising.

The Scojo Foundation works in India, Guatemala and El Salvador, and is just starting out in Bangladesh. It was named Fast Company magazine Social Capitalist of the Year in 2004.

Jordan's story

" Seeing the light

When I was an Optometry student I found out about this organisation which brought eye care to the developing world Volunteer Optometric Services to Humanity (VOSH). To be honest, I had no great calling to go out there and serve the world, but I was 23 years old and this seemed a pretty cool opportunity; I'd get to travel and see other cultures, and yeah it would nice to help out and practice my skills.

So off I went to Merida in Mexico, and my first patient was a six year old boy from a school for the blind. Great I thought, I'm just a first-year student who doesn't know much about anything and I get this really hard case. When I looked at this kid I knew there was something kind of weird, so I pulled over my professor. She looked at him, and she looked at him again, and she looked at me and she said: 'Jordan this kid isn't blind'. We did a full exam and got him the strongest pair of glasses we could find. As we placed those glasses on his eyes, his blank stare changed and this smile came onto his face; he was literally seeing the world for the first time. This boy had been at a school for the blind, living like a blind person, and he was just profoundly nearsighted. That moment for both he and I was magical and profound; it was life changing to see something as simple as a pair of glasses make such an overwhelming difference to someone's life.

A few weeks later I treated a 50 year old lady who was deeply religious but hadn't been able to read her bible for 10 years. All she needed was a pair of reading glasses like the ones you get in Boots for a few pounds, and when we put them on her face there was the same kind of reaction. Suddenly she could read her bible again, and she was so pleased that she gave me a big hug and 20 chickens. All I had done was give her a pair of reading glasses but she told me that I had reconnected her to her God; to me that was pretty profound. Having these kind of experiences made me realise that the skills I was learning at optometry school enabled me to do some pretty cool stuff that could really change lives, and from then on I guess I was kind of addicted to that sort of work.

Refusing to lighten up

Back at university I became president of the VOSH student chapter, and I started to ask some hard questions that others were avoiding: there must be better ways to do this stuff; what happens to that six year old boy if he loses his glasses in two weeks and can't replace them? People were like: 'Lighten up Jordan, we're helping people, doing the best we can, and we're having some fun; we can't save the world'. But those questions really bugged me, so I did some research and found this incredible eye doctor in India called Dr G Venkataswamy, 'Dr V', who had basically created what was, and still is, the finest model of community ophthalmology in the world. I wrote and offered to volunteer my time at his hospital in return for food and lodgings, and he said 'you're on'.

Simple solutions can solve profound problems

I spent the next 12 years before founding Scojo splitting my time between international public health work and having a 'real life' as an eye doctor in New York. During this time I led a project in Africa, for Helen Keller International, distributing a drug called Mectizan (offered for free by Merck) which treated river blindness. We basically just had to figure out how to get this pill into millions of people's mouths because it only took one pill, once a year to combat the disease; it was delivering a really simple health solution to a profound problem. And that's the key theme, that's what I was seeing throughout the 12 years, and it's what led me to found The Scojo Foundation. Sometimes one pill, or one pair of glasses could fundamentally change someone's life. It was just a question of access.

The starting model

So that was the learning on which my business partner Scott Berrie and I based and launched The Scojo Foundation. The overall premise of our idea was that you didn't need eye doctors flying in from America to do things that basically boiled down to a market distribution failure and could be handled by the local population. Our mechanism was simple: select women to become 'Vision Entrepreneurs', train them in basic eye screenings, and provide them with the credit to buy a stock of glasses, that they can then distribute and make money from doing so. We also equipped them to make referrals when they discovered eye problems beyond their training.

We employ women because they tend to be more entrepreneurial, they have a greater need for opportunity, and they use their earnings more responsibly. So, we impact on the lives of our entrepreneurs by providing them with employment, but where we really create change is when they provide their wider community with glasses. In doing so they enable large numbers to enjoy a higher quality of life, and to work for longer; the weavers, tailors, artisans, mechanics, barbers... all those people who need to see up close but have trouble doing so after the age of 40. In this way we often describe The Scojo Foundation as a venture to create and sustain jobs, it just happens to achieve its objectives through the sale of a very useful health product

Evolving in the field

That underlying concept is still what we do, but the detail of how we do it continually evolves and morphs. We used to get our entrepreneurs started through a microcredit loan, but now we give them what we call a 'Business in a Box' which contains the materials, stock, information, even the uniform they need. Being cashless credit it's just less complex and risky for both sides, and because we own the box we can just take it back if things don't work out. Plus we don't spend 80% of our time managing loans as we used to, which isn't our core competency or what we want to be doing.

Other changes come directly from entrepreneurs innovating off their own bat. We used to tell people to sell glasses door-to-door, then we found some women in Guatemala were going into a town, meeting with the elders, the mayor, the pastor, the politician... and explaining that they would come back the following week with 100 pairs of reading glasses to sell. If they were talking to the pastor they'd say 'It'll help people read their bible', if they were talking to the politician they'd say 'It'll help people to continue earning their livelihood as a weaver or a tailor'. Those community leaders would then spend a week marketing for us: the pastor doing the sermon would say 'On Wednesday Margarita is going to be at the school selling reading glasses', the mayor would have people with megaphones announcing Margarita's visit. When Margarita shows up on Wednesday there's a line of 100 people waiting for the service.

With these and countless other tweaks and evolutions we think we've got to a pretty replicable and scaleable model, and trade is now really starting to spike; about 80% of our last three years' sales have come within the last three months.

Combining the for-profit and not-for-profit – for funding and more!

The other important element of Scojo is the combination of a for-profit company and a non-profit foundation. Scojo Vision was launched in New York City to fill a gap in the market between drugstore glasses and designer frames. Before Starbucks coffee was sort of just coffee; similarly ready-made reading glasses was a very tired category that nobody had put any innovation into, and I often saw my patients pull a $10 pair of glasses out of their $2,000 Armani suit. Our 'for-profit' plan in a nutshell was to add fashion to reading glasses, keep them affordable, and capture a previously untapped middle ground. Scojo Vision then donates 5% of its profits to The Scojo Foundation, and one day this cash will be sufficient to cover the overheads of the Foundation, the ugly costs that donors don't want to pay for.

The dynamic is very interesting between the two organisations. When we were starting Scojo Vision and building this quality brand we had to make sure that our product was strong enough to stand alone and that we never depended on our social mission to make sales; for us to be sustainable our glasses had to sell because they were great glasses. In fact the charitable link would even turn some people away from us because they assumed we'd be selling low quality 'charity glasses'. So, initially we kept the for-profit and non-profit stories divorced. Now it's different; we're in Saks 5th Avenue, Neiman Marcus, Bergdorf Goodman... and so our product is strong enough that we can safely leverage the social mission in the marketing of our 'for-profit' company. Maybe we'll stick a little plaque or a picture of an Indian weaver in India on the point of purchase displays; we are still kinda working on that!

Other benefits for Scojo Vision include PR; The Scojo Foundation gets much more exposure than the for-profit side and each time the story is told the brand benefits. In terms of staff we get the very real advantage of a for-profit team being infused by the heart and soul of a foundation; people feel that they work for a business that has a social purpose which is rare and valuable in the commercial world.

Benefits go in a nice back and forth way, and The Scojo Foundation benefits equally from being attached to a for-profit beyond simply the 5% donation. In New York the Foundation has access to Scott, myself, our art director, our innovations team, our book keeper, the knowledge of sourcing and inventories and systems, and we share suppliers which helps get a better deal on stock. I think most importantly however, The Scojo Foundation staff had become infused by the rigor and the discipline of a for-profit company, and that's a quality all too lacking in the voluntary sector. I know that business is not the answer to every problem in the world, but there are many development problems which could benefit from some business thinking, and there are many 'non-profits' which don't know how to replicate or scale because they don't have a business approach to their mission. Hopefully, because of our kind of hybrid existence we'll be well equipped to take The Scojo Foundation to the next level.

Our impact

We measure the impact of The Scojo Foundation based on three goals: selling reading glasses, helping people to start small businesses, and referring patients that have needs beyond the capabilities of our entrepreneurs. What we need to do next is work out how to measure the wider economic impact created by helping the barber or the carpenter or the artisan to work for another 20 years. We need the data to be able to go to a State Minister in India and say: 'Hey, the average person who doesn't have reading glasses loses x amount of productivity a year; multiply that by the x million people in your state who need reading glasses and you'll see that your state is losing $x million every year, simply because your population does not have access to this simple product.' That would be pretty powerful stuff.

We've also got some really compelling anecdotal evidence of our impact from the front line. We have an entrepreneur in El Salvador called Anne Virginia. She owned a small store selling courgettes and other vegetables, but her husband walked out leaving her with four kids, and life got kinda tough. She got on our programme, and despite having no formal education she turned out to be a natural salesperson and entrepreneur; she just can't stop selling glasses and is now our number one salesperson in Latin America. A couple of weekends ago she sold 102 pairs in one weekend and made over $400; that's about a third of her previous annual salary. She has been with us just over a year and has been able to put her kids into school and build another room in her house; her life has just got better.

She now has a few Vision Entrepreneurs working for her, and represents a whole new structure of Super Entrepreneurs who operate like regional sales directors.

In India we had a customer who was a 42 year old goldsmith with failing eyesight. He was losing the ability to do close-up jewellery work and so had to outsource clients to younger goldsmiths, resulting in a 40% drop in his already fairly meagre income. When he found out that one of his friends had become a Vision Entrepreneur he got himself examined, got a pair of reading glasses, and has now recaptured his clients and is back to where he was before his eyesight started to fail. There are tons of people like this goldsmith who are not dying of malaria, not dying of AIDS but who aren't fully whole because of this low lying, ubiquitous condition that everyone gets after the age of 40.

Going forward

Our ultimate goal is a world where nobody loses their livelihood because they don't have access to a simple pair of reading glasses. But 1.5 billion people out there need glasses so we're not going to get there tomorrow, and because we'd need 150 million entrepreneurs to serve that many people we're looking at other distribution channels. One that we're testing in India is what we call the Mobile Unit. We go to locations where there is a concentration of people that tend to need glasses such as lace parks where there are literally dozens and dozens of factories making lacework. We meet with the owners of those factories and say: 'Hey guess what guys? There's a lot of productivity drain going on in your factory because people can't see that well up close. Could we come in and screen your employees and sell them reading glasses?'. So far that's been a great success and there are hundreds of those huge factory complexes throughout the developing world for us to target.

We're also in trials to add our glasses to existing distribution networks. We're working with Hindustan Lever, Unilever's joint venture in India, who has really evolved the marketing of products to people living in poverty through initiatives such as single use sashets for soap, shampoo and toothpaste. In India they have 30,000 women that they call Shakti Ammans who sell Hindustan Lever products across the country and we've just trained 70 of them to start selling our reading glasses. We've got a similar partnership in Bangladesh with BRAC, the largest non-profit in the world who has 20,000 women selling health products. If things go to plan, a year from now we'll have enrolled 500 to 1,000 Shakti Ammans and about the same through Brac, and in five years we should be able to talk in the tens of thousands. Considering we currently have about 150 Vision Entrepreneurs that's a pretty significant expansion.

My top tips

"Find your zone in life. By that I mean find the thing that harnesses your passions, your capabilities, and your virtues and try to spend as much of your time on the things that exercise all of those characteristics. When you find your zone, that space within yourself, things move effortlessly, time passes effortlessly and there is almost a synchronicity in what happens. Once you've tapped into those energies you are passionate about what you do and you love your work. If you can find your zone, your sweet spot, what really drives you, then you are a lucky person. If that zone happens to be helping other people, the world is lucky too."

"In any entrepreneurial venture the important thing is to just start. Don't wait until you have the perfect plan because that will never come. Once you start, you'll see what works and what doesn't, you'll have 80% failure and 20% success, you'll tweak and you'll throw things out, but it's only by starting that you'll build something that will work."

"If you're selling an ethical product or have a charitable link like we do, don't depend too heavily on the marketing notion that people will buy your product because it does good. Prove yours to be the best product in the marketplace, and only then leverage all the great work you are doing."

My call to action

"Governments need to realise that social entrepreneurship is a powerful tool for development; it's the old teach them to fish thing, and it's what good development really is. More government development dollars need to go towards social enterprise rather than just relief."

Ideas you can steal

Ask tough questions of traditional solutions

It's not enough to simply be 'doing good', and traditional charity or humanitarian solutions shouldn't be thought of as untouchable just because they're well-intentioned. When Jordan returned from his development work as a student, despite being pretty young, he challenged the traditional methods he had encountered. In our opinion he has emerged with something comprehensively more impactful.

Growing up means evolving

Scojo has always welcomed inspiration to change; they continually look to the field for better ways of doing things and are very open to noticing when things could be better. They've stayed wedded to their underlying goal of getting glasses out into the world, but are flexible as to how they should achieve this.

Share and share alike

Scojo has recognised the importance of sharing the qualities from the for-profit and non-profit sectors in a way that equips both sides of Scojo to do great things. The commercial arm is infused with pride and satisfaction that they are about more than a financial bottom line, and the foundation has become instilled with a discipline and dynamism that is all too often lacking in the traditional world of development and charity.

Hide your ugly bits

Scojo cleverly use their donation from the for-profit company to fund the Foundation costs in New York City. Often people don't want their donation to fund rents or salaries, so donor cash is ring-fenced for the development of new projects in the field.

Getting off the sofa! Acting on inspiration

We hope you've been inspired by the stories and people in this book. Even better would be if you were resolved to try something similar yourself. We're not suggesting that everyone throws in their jobs and dedicates themselves to a lifetime of social entrepreneurship; there's a sliding scale from simply doing more recycling through to launching your own social enterprise with many impactful things in-between. Whichever point on the scale you start, it's all about the fact that you've made a start, and who knows where it might lead? We want you to find where your passions lie, and then take on what works for you.

What you might find is that once the immediate surge of inspiration has passed it's difficult to get it back. It's amazing how everyday life can become a barrier to what you originally wanted to do; work, money, time, routine all get in the way of your plans; they clog up the essential sense of momentum. To help you maintain your momentum there are a couple of things you need to keep in mind:

Don't wait for your idea to be perfect

An idea will never be fully formed before you try it out, once you've started it will naturally evolve and improve. Many of the stories we've told involve a moment of spontaneous action; Eric saw that there was no fresh fruit and veg available on his estate so he bought wholesale produce and sold it on to local residents; Carmel discovered that kids were going to school too hungry to learn so she started serving breakfast foods in a school. Don't wait too long before you start to act; it's far better to try things out and see where they take you.

Keep stimulating your mind

When you're looking to start making a difference it's very difficult to come up with new ideas; this is because our brains are naturally geared towards us learning from past experiences. As people we're set up to become very good at what we 'do'. We're trained to totally master a task whether it be accountancy, looking

126

after children or driving a cab. In one sense this is highly effective; it allows us to make quick decisions and take short cuts at the drop of a hat. It means we develop what we call a 'river of thinking'; the more you know about an area the faster and deeper your river flows. But, it also means the harder it is to get out.

To come up with new solutions you have to get out of your river, and this generally takes a bit of a jolt. You need a piece of stimulus that tells you how other people have approached an issue, and which you can learn from. It's just lateral thinking. We want you to consider this book as stimulus to help you come up with your own new ideas about how you can help to tackle social issues. The important thing is that having read the book you don't stop here, you look for more stimulus. Look at other people, at other worlds, cultures and sectors and see what ideas this generates.

This ties into a key principle of social entrepreneurship, and it goes back to our diagram on page 4; colliding different worlds, bringing together people of different mindsets, combining business skills with a social conscience, and not taking traditional solutions as the only way to go. There are better ideas out there to create positive change, they just haven't been thought of yet!

A big thank you to…

Sandra Jetten (UnLtd) and Kristina Murrin (?What If!) who were the
brains behind this book, and the partners at ?What If! who fund
?What If! Footprint and put the cash up for the project.

Rachel Slade who compiled Bob's chapter beautifully and quickly,
Chloe Martin our resident photographer, Ed Herten whose sharp mind helped
shape the original concept, Christian Eldridge for helping to inspire the
design process, and Adrian Simpson who generously opened the
?What If! Inspiration team's address book.

Thanks also to…

Adam Bedford, Angharad Barton, Atif Sheikh, Bob Sheridan, Claire Hillier,
Emma Rea, Jon Allen, Jonathan Kemp, Katie Griggs, Krystian Taylor, Lauren
Daniels, Rebecca Potter, Sukh Bhathal, Shabana Pathan and Zoe Daniels who
helped us in various different ways throughout the project. They're all staff
from UnLtd and ?What If!, two really inspiring places to work.

A 'not forgetting thanks' to…

The Millennium Commission for enabling UnLtd to support so many
fantastic social entrepreneurs. The Millennium Awards Trust was endowed
by the Millennium Commission with a National Lottery grant of £100million as
a permanent source of grants for individuals throughout the United Kingdom
to develop their own skills and talents and to contribute to the community.

And of course special thanks to…

All the people whose stories we've featured, and the teams that support them.
Without them this book would obviously be a bit thin.